CW00712922

BIXOLOGY

# BIXOLOGY

## COCKTAILS, CULTURE, AND A GUIDE TO THE GOOD LIFE

BY

EVE O'NEILL AND DOUG "BIX" BIEDERBECK

PHOTOGRAPHS BY SHERI GIBLIN

ILLUSTRATIONS BY BENOÎT VAN INNIS

CHRONICLE BOOKS
SAN FRANCISCO

Library of Congress Cataloging-in-Publication Data available.

ISBN 978-0-8118-6707-8

Manufactured in the United States of America

Design by Hallie Overman, Brooklyn, New York

Page 158 constitutes a continuation of the copyright page.

10 9 8 7 6 5 4 3 2 1

Chronicle Books LLC
680 Second Street
San Francisco, California 94107

www.chroniclebooks.com

# TABLE OF CONTENTS

# ON THE HOUSE

In 1987 we came upon an abandoned restaurant on Gold Street, an alley in San Francisco's Jackson Square. It reeked of dead restaurant and had been savagely stripped of anything remotely saleable. Piles of debris sat in the middle of the dining room. The place had once been a restaurant that celebrated New Year's Eve every night of the year—we found the sad little tiaras and top hats given out to patrons as we cleaned out the previous tenant's wares. Still, it had good bones. There were voluminous ceilings, ornate moldings, and a layout that really could work for a restaurant. I had been mulling over plans for a supper club for some time, and I knew right away that this was the place.

We hired an architect, Michael Guthrie, and planned what would soon come to be called "Bix," mostly in honor of Bix Beiderbecke, a justly celebrated jazz coronet player who died at the ripe old age of twenty-eight in 1931. He fell victim to pneumonia, but hard living and bathtub gin probably hastened his early departure from the bandstand. My last name is Biederbeck, and though my family is not related to the musician, I nevertheless picked up the nickname "Bix," as had my father before me. Since our restaurant was going to feature live jazz, we decided to trade on my nickname and Bix's reputation.

"Supper club" is a bit of a misnomer, since we never planned to have shows and we weren't going to charge cover fees. We wanted guests to be able to listen, drink, eat, and talk all at the same time. But the feel and look of the room said "updated supper club," and we've used that moniker ever since.

We took lots of influences from the jazz era. We were the first West Coast restaurant to respark the current Martini boom. It's a little hard to imagine that, only twenty years ago, the white-wine spritzer, gin and tonic, and occasional sweet drink were the calls of choice. The Cosmopolitan had only recently been invented, and there were about six vodkas known to man. Wine by the glass was limited to crude generic offerings from unknown wine factories.

I insisted (at some expense) that the restaurant be comfortable. Our booths were a little firmer, a little larger, and covered in an expensive Clarence House fabric. Our mahogany bar was built in one piece in Santa Rosa, California, by a boatbuilder. When the bar arrived by truck for installation, the only way it made it into the restaurant was because its curve allowed us to finesse it in through the front door. The alley we are located in is so narrow that a straight bar wouldn't have been able to turn the corner.

We put a menu together of what we thought of as classic supper club dishes—things like steak tartare and chicken hash. We always offered a plate of cold shellfish, and, in season, garden tomatoes. We never intended to forge a new cuisine, because we were confident that comfort food had its place. The goal was to be satisfying and yet different. Bix was a swanky, moody room full of music and paintings—who wouldn't want to drop by after the theater, in their tuxedos and gowns, for a great hamburger and an exceptional bottle of Burgundy? Our aim has always been to embrace both high and low, the raffish with the rarified.

We got very lucky—and have remained so—with our musicians. We have live music every evening. For many years, we had an exquisite trio made up of pianist Merrill Hoover (Anita O'Day's favorite pianist when in San Francisco), bassist Wyatt Ruther (an old acquaintance of Thelonious Monk), and the elegant tenor-sax man Benny Miller (who played with Duke Ellington and other greats). Sadly, that original trio is gone, but we are still lucky to have the great Mary Stallings on vocals. Mary sang with Count Basie early in her career and has had a devoted clientele ever since. When she isn't busy selling out venues in Japan or the Village Vanguard in New York, Mary can be found at Bix, having her way with jazz standards accompanied by George Khouri, our unfailingly polite musical director. Her version of Johnny Mercer's "Drinking Again" is not to be missed. I think of it as our song. (I probably shouldn't mention that I turned Harry Connick Jr. down as "not ready yet" when his agent sent me an audition tape many years ago.)

I am often asked why Bix has been so successful for so long. For one thing, we are a little hard to find. Secluded from the main streets but located just off an accessible one, we are in an alley only one block long, which means we kind of own it. People love to tell their friends that Bix is hard to find but that they know where it is. Our space is not big—the dining room seats one hundred—but it has a volume and a scale that hit just the right balance between intimacy and excitement.

Someone once told me that people feel as if they can take ownership of Bix; it has that aura of fantasy. You can make Bix fit whatever your mental picture of the Jazz Age is. It's dark and comfortable, and I get the feeling that people find it acceptable to have one more glass of Champagne here than they usually do. But the secret to our success has probably been the mix of customers. If Bix is not a restaurant for the ages, it is certainly a restaurant for all ages . . . at least any age that can order a cocktail. For every diner who recalls the original supper club era there is a tech-savvy thirtysomething with a gang of friends at the bar. Some of our guests have never sat in our dining room, yet our bartenders know their birthdays. Out-of-towners celebrating big events sit next to locals who use Bix as a canteen. Everyone mingles. Everyone gets along. The mix keeps us fresh, ever-changing, and, in a way, liberated from the need to "catch the next wave." We strive for currency in our approach to dining, but with great respect for what has worked in the past.

So why "bixology"? Maybe I mean "bixography." After twenty years and countless memorable experiences, we thought it worthwhile to gather, in one bound book, the many influences, inspirations, and experiences that have formed the culture of Bix Restaurant. That particular culture dictates our way of doing things and our sense of purpose. I'm not sure I could ever describe this culture, but it all tucks nicely under the heading of bixology—our way of looking at the world through the eyes of a restaurant. In this book you won't find hundreds of recipes or a list of forty-five different rum drinks. You will find the recipe for the last-minute cocktail party you need to throw together, and that same recipe might include a recommendation for music to help along the mood and bons mots to sprinkle like salted nuts in front of your guests. Having a party every night has taught us a lot about choices: There are too many in this world, so you should concentrate on a few good ones.

It goes without saying that we owe an awful lot of thanks to an awful lot of people. I offer mine in equal parts to our many wonderful guests and our devoted, loyal staff. I am lucky to serve and work with such a terrific group. Special thanks, too, to the farmers, winemakers, artists, musicians, and writers who have added to the culture here on Gold Street. Finally, this book—talked about, promised, and threatened for several years—wouldn't be in your hands without its author, Eve O'Neill.

☛ DOUG "BIX" BIEDERBECK

## THE RULES DEFINED BY DECADES OF MIXING ARE SIMPLE AND FEW:

**1.** Use fresh ingredients.
**2.** Chill well—all drinks, even bad ones, taste better ice-cold.
**3.** Avoid drinks that come in colors not found in nature.
**4.** If it doesn't taste like alcohol, it's not a proper cocktail.

When cartoonist R. Crumb ate at Bix, it was the only time in the history of the restaurant that butcher paper may "accidentally" have graced the table ☛

# SALUTATIONS, CELEBRATIONS, AND REPARATIONS

**WORK IS THE CURSE OF THE DRINKING CLASSES.**

☞ OSCAR WILDE

Classic cocktails have changed little in nearly two centuries of existence, though where and when the practice of blending spirits, wines, and juices started remains a topic of debate. In America, the mixing of drinks began sometime in the 1800s, ironically thrived during the Prohibition years, and created cultural icons in the latter half of the twentieth century.

Mixed drinks are as prolific and lunatic as their inventors, but do you really want to invite your friends over for a round of Flaming Ferraris? We didn't think so. In admiration of America's long tradition of drinks, and in respect for their drinkers, we have included ten of our recipes for classic cocktails, the greatest of which—invented by accident or necessity—require little more than a scoop of ice, twenty seconds in a cocktail shaker, and a willing victim.

There is a reason Hemingway looked into a daiquiri and saw the waves of the Caribbean, or why pastis remains the French aperitif of choice almost a century after its invention. If prepared well, these ten essentials can provide for a lifetime of pleasurable drinking.

**A.** The molecular formula of ethanol is $C_2H_5OH$.

**B.** *Proof* is the measure of how much ethanol is in a spirit. In America, a drink's "degree of proof" is twice the percentage of its alcohol content by volume (ABV). Therefore, 80 proof is 40 percent ABV. Pure alcohol is 200 proof. In the eigthteenth century, British sailors were often paid in rum for their troubles. The sailors would "prove" the rum's potency by mixing it with gunpowder and seeing if the mixture ignited. One hundred degrees of proof—or approximately 50 percent ABV—was the flash point.

The navy certainly got their hands on more than just rum. Turn to page 41 ☞

**C.** Shaken Martinis and stirred ones are chemically distinct. The University of Western Ontario's biochemistry department once conducted a study to determine if the antioxidant capacity of a gin Martini was altered by different methods of preparation. Its findings revealed that "a stirred gin Martini left behind 0.157 percent peroxide." A shaken Martini was able to break down hydrogen peroxide in gin more effectively, "leaving only 0.072 percent of the peroxide behind," therefore perhaps "containing stronger antioxidant properties than a Martini of the stirred variety." Why not try your Martini both ways to see which you prefer? You'll undoubtedly have the most popular booth at the next science fair.

At this point, James Bond lovers may turn to page 58 ☞

## PERFECT MANHATTAN

The Manhattan has been around forever. Its longevity can be attributed to the simple way in which the meltwater from the ice changes the flavor profile of the alcohol, much in the way wine responds to oxygen. What makes this drink "perfect" is the use of both sweet and dry vermouth. This cocktail can effectively cure anyone with an aversion to whiskey.

| | |
|---|---|
| 1½ ounces rye whiskey | ¼ ounce dry vermouth |
| ¼ ounce sweet vermouth | 1 to 2 drops Angostura bitters |

Combine all ingredients in a cocktail shaker over ice and stir or shake gently. Strain into a chilled stemmed glass. Garnish with a cherry.

Note . . . Shaking your Manhattan vigorously in a cocktail shaker will overdilute the drink; gently rocking it back and forth will do the trick. You could even forgo shaking entirely and try stirring your ingredients instead. Try making your Manhattan with Carpano Antica, the original Italian sweet vermouth. Slightly drier, it will add a little weight to the drink.

One shot  ☞  44.3602943 milliliters  ☞  1½ ounces

## SEVEN BAR GLASSES

ROCKS GLASS

MARTINI/COCKTAIL

HIGHBALL

SLING/
COLLINS

SNIFTER

LIQUEUR

WHEN ALL ELSE FAILS

There are many ways to remedy what ails us. Sometimes you need sleep and chicken soup. Sometimes you just need a stiff drink. Many of the ingredients used in cocktails originated as just that—medicinal tonics or digestive aids.

**ANGOSTURA BITTERS** In 1824 a German physician in Venezuela developed Angostura aromatic bitters flavored with gentian root, a common digestive tonic. A little bottle with a comically oversized label, the result of a factory error made in the 1800s, gentian bitters are still reputed to settle mild cases of nausea and stimulate the appetite. They can be used in just about anything, from gin to rum drinks, whiskey to Champagne.

**FERNET-BRANCA** Fernet-Branca was created by Maria Scala (her married name was Branca) in 1845 in Milan. Its extensive list of ingredients is still a secret. Fernet-Branca was once used to treat cholera. Every once in a while someone will order Fernet as an after-dinner digestif, but ask any bartender for their favorite hangover cure (and they are well versed in such things), and chances are, it will be a shot of Fernet.

**JÄGERMEISTER** The German word *jägermeister* means "master hunter," a title once given to senior foresters. One of Hermann Göring's titles under the Nazi regime was Reichsjägermeister (master of the Reich's hunters), and since Jägermeister as we know it today was created in 1934, it is speculated that the brew was created to honor Göring. It is occasionally referred to as

Leberkleister ("liver glue"), and may have been used as a field anesthetic in World War II. Perhaps this will help you stimulate some conversation while attending your next frat party.

**CHARTREUSE** The exact recipes for all the forms of Chartreuse are known only to the three monks who prepare the herbal mixture. The formula purportedly contains 130 herbs, flowers, and secret ingredients combined in a wine-alcohol base. The monks intended their liqueur to be used as medicine.

**TONIC/QUININE WATER** Tonic is a common mixer for spirits, but true to its name, it was first used as a treatment for malaria in South Asia and Africa. The slight bitterness in tonic water comes from quinine, bark from the South American cinchona tree.

## CALORIC TABLE

Ladies and gents wishing to preserve their winsome figures may consult this handy table reflecting calories per ounce.

| | |
|---|---|
| **BEER** | 10–16 |
| **CHAMPAGNE** | 26–28 |
| **LIQUEUR** | 85–105 |
| **SPIRITS** | 65–74 |
| **WINE** | 22–24 |

### LILLET

An aperitif from France, Lillet comes in two varieties. Golden-colored Lillet Blanc tastes honeyed and slightly floral, while Lillet Rouge has the subtle flavors of berries, vanilla, and spice. Serve either variety chilled—alone, over ice, or topped with soda water.

### PIMM'S NO. 1 AND LEMONADE

Mix lemonade and Pimm's, three to one, in a pitcher filled with ice. Add slices of orange, lemon, apple, or cucumber and perhaps a few mint leaves.

Note . . . Invented in a London oyster bar in the 1840s, Pimm's originally came in six different styles. Only three continue to be produced:

**PIMM'S No.1**.........is gin based
**No.2**..........was whiskey based
**No.3**...............is brandy based
         (produced seasonally)

**No.4**..................was rum based
**No.5**....................was rye based
**No.6**...................is vodka based
         (quite rare)

Heading back to the office? Try our quick recipes for simple summer refreshment without the kick on page 50 ☛

## SIDECAR

The Sidecar is a great example of a drink in which a little bit of style goes a long way. Use a good brandy and you'll find the difference in the final cocktail to be notable. We like Germain-Robin, a modern American brandy distilled in a traditional alembic still.

1½ ounces Germain-Robin brandy
¾ ounce Cointreau

Splash of sweet-and-sour (see opposite)
Juice of ½ lime

Shake ingredients vigorously with ice. Strain into a stemmed glass with a sugar rim. Garnish with a lime wheel.

Tip: Using a dry cocktail glass, as opposed to one that is fogged from the freezer or wet from the dishwasher, will yield a precise sugar rim that doesn't spread all over the glass, thus helping you avoid sticky fingers and oversweetening your drink. Simply moisten the outside rim of the glass with a wedge of lime—no dipping it into a plate of lime juice—then turn it over and lightly press the top of the glass into a shallow dish of sugar. Also, keep the level of your cocktail below the rim rather than pouring it all the way to the top. The idea is to have the tart lime and brandy sweetened only once—as you drink. If you get sugar on the inside of the glass, it will combine with the cocktail, and all of that wonderful brandy flavor will be lost.

**TO MAKE THE SWEET-AND-SOUR:**

Fresh juice transforms a drink. Try this simple recipe for sweet-and-sour and give up your addiction to premade mixers here and now:

| | | |
|---|---|---|
| 1½ cups fresh lemon juice | ‖ | ⅔ cup simple syrup |
| 1½ cups water | ‖ | (see below) |

Stir ingredients together in a pitcher. Juice from fresh lemons will keep for about one week.

Note . . . Simple syrup can be bought, but it's just as easy to make and will keep in your fridge for several weeks. Combine two parts sugar to one part water in a saucepan over low heat. Heat the mixture until all the sugar dissolves. Remove from heat and let cool.

MYTH: Amaretto is an almond liqueur.

TRUTH: Amaretto is not distilled from almonds. It's made from apricot pits steeped in brandy or another neutral spirit. Herbs and sweeteners are then added to give amaretto its recognizable flavor.

**BRUT**...................................................very dry (the most popular style)

**EXTRA SEC**.................................................................extra dry

**SEC**.................................................................moderately sweet

**DEMI-SEC**..........................................................distinctly sweet

**DOUX**.............................................very sweet, more like dessert wine

**BLANC DE BLANC** Champagne can be made from several different grape varietals. If it is made from 100 percent chardonnay grapes, however, it is then labeled "blanc de blanc."

**BLANC DE NOIR** A type of Champagne made from either pinot noir or pinot meunier varietals. No chardonnay is used in a blanc de noir.

**CUVÉE** The French word *cuvée* means "vat" or "tank," and Champagne houses use *cuvée* as a general term to refer to all the wine they are making. Many houses use terms such as *tête de cuvée* and *prestige cuvée* to refer to particularly exceptional pressings, and often market these pressings separately. Roederer's prestige cuvée is Cristal. Moët & Chandon's prestige cuvée is Dom Pérignon.

**A BOTTLE OF CHAMPAGNE CONTAINS 750 ML OF LIQUID.**

The French have appropriated the names of biblical kings to refer to quantities of grander scale:

**SPLIT**..................................................................................½ bottle
**MAGNUM**...........................................................................2 bottles
**JEROBOAM**.........................................................................4 bottles
**REHOBOAM**.........................................................................6 bottles
**METHUSELAH**.....................................................................8 bottles
**SALAMANZAR**.........................................................10 or 12 bottles
**BALTHAZAR**.......................................................................16 bottles
**NEBUCHADNEZZAR**............................................................20 bottles

While you expand your repertoire of Champagne terminology, why not sip a Champagne cocktail. Kindly turn the page 👉

## CHAMPAGNE COCKTAIL

A Champagne cocktail is the ideal party drink. A tray of them fools your guests into thinking you actually made some effort. It's also a festive way to serve modestly priced sparklers, or get rid of the bottle you've had sitting in your cabinet since last Christmas.

| | |
|---|---|
| 1 sugar cube | Champagne or sparkling wine |
| 2 dashes Angostura bitters | |

Soak the sugar cube with the bitters. Pour Champagne into a flute and drop the sugar cube in last. Garnish with a twist of lemon.

Note . . . By dropping your sugar cube in last, you avoid the big foamy mess that occurs when you pour Champagne over sugar already sitting in the glass.

At Bix, we like to pair the grand with the gauche. For the perfect foil to this elegant cocktail, turn to page 122 ☞

Toasting is a practice that originated in ancient Greece due to rampant fears of poisoning. To ensure the safety of the beverage in question, a host would pour everyone's drink from the same bottle, sample his own glass, and raise his cup to invite everyone to drink at the same time. Toasts should be made to health, friendship—or more drinking. Three handy standbys:

**TO HEALTH**

May we get what we want, may we get what we need,
but may we never get what we deserve.

☞ TRADITIONAL IRISH TOAST

**TO FRIENDSHIP**

Let us toast your enemies' enemies!

☞ ANONYMOUS

**TO DRINKING**

Man, being reasonable, must get drunk;
The best of life is but intoxication.

☞ LORD GEORGE GORDON BYRON

An ancient superstition states that when you clink two glasses together you scare the demon out of the alcohol. Still suspicious? You're not the only one. Turn to page 87 ☞

## CAIPIRINHA

Cachaça (ka-SHA-sa) is the vodka of Brazil, and the Caipirinha (keye-peh-REEN-ya) is the country's most famous cocktail. Cachaça is distilled from sugarcane juice, and if you ever happen to stumble upon a bar that makes its Caipirinha with freshly pressed sugarcane, make sure you try it, as this makes for an incredible taste. Originally a cheap peasant drink, cachaça is still used as a crude substitute for fuel in some parts of the country. Typically the spirit is not aged, though as its reputation improves, this is beginning to change.

| | |
|---|---|
| 6 to 8 lime wedges | 1½ ounces cachaça |
| 1 teaspoon superfine sugar | |

Muddle the limes and the sugar in the bottom of a large rocks glass. Fill with ice, add cachaça, and stir. Do not strain.

---

First you take a drink,
Then the drink takes a drink,
Then the drink takes you.

☞ F. SCOTT FITZGERALD

## NEGRONI

Nothing says "grown-up" like a Negroni. Citrus flavors and gin are an unbeatable combination. Rather than using a fruit juice, the drink gets its kick from the bitterness of the Campari.

¾ ounce Damrak gin  ¾ ounce sweet vermouth
¾ ounce Campari

Shake ingredients with ice and strain into a chilled stemmed glass. Garnish with an orange twist.

Note . . . Campari a little too intense for you? Substitute Aperol, Campari with training wheels. An Italian aperitif made by the same company, Aperol is slightly less bitter than Campari but has the same citrus-herbal taste. It makes a suitable substitute for the stronger Campari.

If gin makes you deliciously rummy, also try holding a rickey or a Collins in your hand—kindly turn to page 42 ☞

Some people have an uncanny resemblance to their pets. Others, to their drinks. A few famous political figures have come down with this affliction:

| | |
|---|---|
| **GERALD FORD** | Gin and Tonic |
| **HERBERT HOOVER** | Martini |
| **RICHARD NIXON** | Rum and Coke |
| **FRANKLIN ROOSEVELT** | Scotch or Brandy |
| **NAPOLEON BONAPARTE** | Scotch |
| **HARRY TRUMAN** | Bourbon |
| **QUEEN ELIZABETH II** | Gin and Tonic |
| **LYNDON JOHNSON** | Scotch and Soda |

## PUB CHEAT SHEET

ALE: Ales come in a range of colors. Pale ales contain dried malts; amber and red ales are made with roasted malts.

BOCK: German for "strong beer," Bock usually has some bitterness and high alcohol content.

LAGER: Light in body and flavor.

PORTER: A richly malted, dark brown beer.

STOUT: Near black in color, with intense body and flavor.

**1.** The body of a whiskey is determined in part by the size of the grain from which it is made: The larger the grain, the lighter the whiskey. Rye is a very small grain; therefore, rye whiskey tends to be much fuller-bodied than, say, bourbon, whose primary ingredient is corn, a larger grain.

**2.** At one time, all whiskey was spelled without the *e.* Around 1870, the proliferation of cheaper products in the market caused the reputation of Scottish whisky to plummet. Irish and American distilleries wished to distinguish their higher-quality product from the Scottish rotgut, and began spelling the name of their product "whiskey." That tradition is continued today.

**3.** Peat is decayed vegetable matter that is commonly used as a fuel source in both the Scottish highlands and Ireland. Peat influences the flavor of whiskey in many ways: either directly, such as using peat in the kiln during malting, or in more subtle ways, such as using water that picks up flavors from the peat over which it flows. Island and coastal peat produces smoke with a much stronger aroma than peat from further inland. Irish whiskey, with rare exception, is never peated.

**4.** Bourbon whiskey, America's only native spirit, was born of necessity—specifically the necessity to find a replacement for rum. When the British navy blockaded the import of sugar and molasses to the American colonies, spirits distilled from native grains began replacing liquor distilled from these imports in much greater quantities. Farmers also had an interest in preserving as much of their harvest as possible, and it cost more to transport grain to the East Coast than it would sell for, so they distilled their surplus corn into an asset that would keep.

**5.** In order to be labeled "bourbon," a whiskey MUST

☞ be made in the United States

☞ consist of at least 51 percent corn

☞ be aged in new, American, charred oak barrels

Those readers desirous of sensory confirmation of the above may turn to pages 19 ☜ and 53 ☞ and follow the directions precisely.

**Q:** If you make a Manhattan with scotch instead of bourbon, what drink have you created?

A. Roy Rodgers    |||    C. Old Fashioned
B. Scotch Martini    |||    D. Rob Roy

See answer, page 156

Fortifying wine began as a necessity at the beginning of the sixteenth century, since the wines at the time did not keep as they were being shipped around the world. The addition of brandy or some other spirit helped prevent them from going bad. The most common types of fortified wine are vermouth (from France and Italy), Marsala (from Italy), sherry (from Spain), and Madeira and port (from Portugal). All are commonly enjoyed neat as aperitifs or after-dinner drinks, though vermouth is widely used as a cocktail mixer as well. Try your hand at these two variations of our classic cocktails.

## PUNT E MES NEGRONI

Somewhere between sweet vermouth and Campari lies Punt e Mes, a slightly bitter Italian vermouth.

¾ ounce gin
¾ ounce sweet vermouth

¾ ounce Punt e Mes

Shake ingredients with ice and strain into a chilled stemmed glass. Garnish with an orange twist.

## FINO SHERRY MARTINI

Try using a very dry (fino) sherry in your Martini in place of dry vermouth. Though a subtle variation, sherry can add the right degree of complexity to a Martini without ruining the trademark simplicity of the drink's few ingredients.

2 ounces dry gin ||| ¼ ounce fino sherry

Shake ingredients with ice in a cocktail shaker and strain into a chilled martini glass. Garnish with olives, onions, or a lemon twist.

For those who like to further tinker with their classics, get started in the kitchen on page 110 ☞

## LA FLORIDITA DAIQUIRI

Named for Ernest Hemingway's favorite bar in Havana, the La Floridita Daiquiri is distinguished by the addition of maraschino liqueur. It takes a bit of finesse to add the essence of the Italian cherry liqueur to the bouquet and body of the cocktail. You may want to try making a daiquiri without the liqueur to note the distinct difference between the two.

1¼ ounces light rum (if you have Havana Club from Cuba, use it— we use Flor de Caña from Nicaragua)

Juice of ½ lime

½ teaspoon superfine sugar (which dissolves better than granulated sugar)

Cautious dash of Luxardo Maraschino Liqueur

Fill a glass with crushed ice. Add all ingredients and stir. Garnish with a lime wheel.

Note . . . If you shake your daiquiri, you'll find a lot of the ice melts quickly, resulting in a watery drink. If you use ice cubes instead of crushed ice, you could get away with giving your ingredients a good shake.

Double the rum content and you have the version favored by Ernest Hemingway. To find other famous writers' drinks of choice, kindly turn to page 54 ☞

Arbiters of civilized etiquette for centuries, sailors gave birth to some of our most common drinking terms:

**ON THE ROCKS:** An expression alluding to the unfortunate condition of being grounded on a rocky coast. The phrase started appearing on bar menus in the 1920s, when it came to refer to the now-common method of serving a drink with ice in the glass.

**TORPEDO JUICE:** These days "torpedo juice" is a catchall term for any homemade whiskey. Originally, though, it was an invention of World War II sailors, who drained grain alcohol from the engines used to propel the ship's torpedoes.

**LIMEY:** The British navy began using lime juice as far back as 1795 to prevent scurvy (vitamin C deficiency), among myriad other ailments related to the unsanitary conditions of life at sea. This American slang for a British sailor came into use about fifty years later.

**THREE SHEETS TO THE WIND:** A sheet is the rope or chain used to shorten or extend a sail. If the sheets are loosened, the ship's sails are free to flap and flutter in the wind. Someone only slightly drunk had "one sheet to the wind." If you were "three sheets to the wind," you could barely steer.

Rickeys and Collinses are two types of cocktails that can be made with any spirit, though we commonly use gin. The difference between the two drinks is a single ingredient.

### RICKEY

2 ounces gin
Juice of ½ lime

||| ½ ounce simple syrup
(recipe on page 25)

Combine in a collins glass with ice and stir. Top with soda, and garnish with a lime.

Note . . . You can add any fruit you like to your rickey. We use everything from strawberries to mangos while in season. Combining the ingredients with lime and topping with soda is what defines the rickey.

Seasonal ingredients make great cocktails. Arm yourself with the chart on page 126 and make a break for the produce section ☛

## COLLINS

2 ounces gin
Juice of ½ lemon

½ ounce simple syrup
(recipe on page 25)

Combine in a collins glass with ice and stir. Top with soda.
Garnish with a cherry and a lemon twist.

Note . . . You can also choose to substitute sweet-and-sour for
the simple syrup and lemon juice. Fruit is not traditionally mixed
with Collinses.

A man's got to believe in something.
I believe I'll have another drink.

☛ W. C. FIELDS

**1.** The word *tequila*. This is how you know it's not rum.

**2.** A "NOM" number. This is the distillery's ID number, and every tequila made in Mexico will have one.

**3.** The age of the tequila, indicated as either *blanco, reposado,* or *añejo. Blanco* means unaged. *Reposado* tequilas are aged in barrels for a minimum of two months. *Añejo* is tequila that has been aged one year or more. These words correspond somewhat vaguely to the color of the drink, which ranges from clear to amber.

**4.** A picture. Ideally a cactus, a sunset, or something appropriately meditative.

**5.** The words "100 percent agave." This phrase is what indicates that what's in the bottle is not agave spirit blended with some other spirit (such as rum, used widely in cheap tequila) or additional sugar.

Looking for a different twist on a classic tequila drink? Turn to page 61 ☛

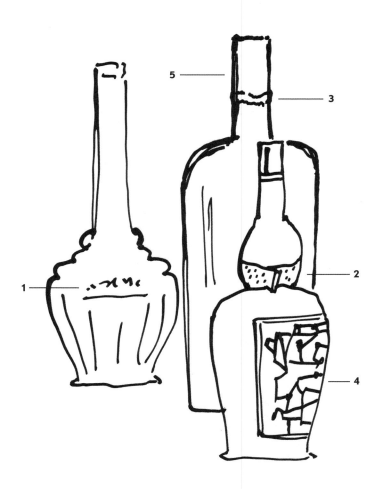

5 ——————

3

1 ——————

2

4

**ORDINARY RED WINE:**
*le gros rouge qui tache et qui pousse au crime*

**LITERAL TRANSLATION:**
the thick red wine that stains and incites to crime

**LUSH:** *une éponge*

**LITERAL TRANSLATION:** a sponge

**THE BILL / THE DAMAGE:** *la douleureuse*

**LITERAL TRANSLATION:** the painful one

Aimez-vous le pastis? Mais oui! Tournez à la page 56 🖝

## GODS OF WINE

| | |
|---|---|
| **GREEK** | Dionysus |
| **ROMAN** | Bacchus |
| **EGYPTIAN** | Osiris |
| **BABYLONIAN** | Adon |

## FOURTEEN TERMS FOR THE TONGUE-TIED WINE TASTER

| | |
|---|---|
| Yeast | Grass |
| Tobacco | Earth |
| Smoke | Cherry |
| Plum | Cedar |
| Pepper | Chocolate |
| Oak | Apple |
| Licorice | Apricot |

## FIVE MORE WINE DESCRIPTORS, SLIGHTLY STRANGER

| | |
|---|---|
| Lead pencil | Leather |
| Rubber | Bacon fat |
| Bell pepper | |

Always do sober what you said you would do drunk.
That will teach you to keep your mouth shut.

☞ ERNEST HEMINGWAY

Humans will distill anything they can get their hands on, but there are alternatives to the tedious sprouting and fermenting of grains. Caffeine is a plant alkaloid that is far simpler to extract and provides much more instant gratification.

CAFFEINE MOLECULE:

| DRINK | CAFFEINE PER SERVING |
|---|---|
| **GREEN TEA, LOOSE** (5 min. brew, 5 ounces) | 20 mg |
| **BLACK TEA, IN BAG** (5 ounces) | 50 mg |
| **COFFEE LIQUEUR** (63 proof, 5 ounces) | 39 mg |
| **COFFEE BREWED FROM GROUNDS** (5 ounces) | 80–100 mg |
| **ESPRESSO** (1 ounce) | 64 mg |
| **DECAFFEINATED COFFEE** (5 ounces) | 3 mg |
| **EXCEDRIN** (1 pill) | 65 mg |
| **DARK CHOCOLATE** (1 ounce) | 20–26 mg |
| **GUARANA BEANS** | twice the caffeine of coffee beans |
| **COCA-COLA** (12 ounces) | 45 mg |

## IRISH COFFEE

Here's a convenient way to combine your addictions.

| | |
|---|---|
| 1½ ounces Irish whiskey | 6 ounces hot coffee |
| 1 teaspoon brown sugar | Heavy, unsweetened cream |

Combine the whiskey, sugar, and coffee in a mug, and stir to dissolve sugar. Shake the cream in a cocktail shaker until thick. Float the cream on top, being careful not to mix it with the coffee. Not only does this look better, but the cream is there to cool the warm drink before it hits your mouth.

"Black Coffee" by Peggy Lee is sure to get you going. Turn to page 94 for other stimulating musical accompaniment ☞

Sadly, though perhaps wisely, the Arnold Palmer has replaced the three-Martini lunch. Mix iced tea and lemonade, fifty-fifty, for a refreshing, work-friendly libation, or try a few other twists to this summertime staple:

**1.** Steep tea with fresh mint, strain leaves, and let cool. Garnish with lemon wheels.

**2.** Add diced fresh melon—honeydew, cantaloupe, watermelon—to brewed tea.

**3.** Steep 2 quarts tea with 1 teaspoon grated fresh ginger. Strain and let cool. Garnish with lime wheels.

**4.** For Thai iced tea, steep 4 to 5 cardamom pods in a quart of hot black tea for 5 minutes. Strain and let cool. Fill ice-filled glasses three-quarters full with tea. Stir in 1 teaspoon sugar and ½ teaspoon cinnamon. Fill glass to top with evaporated milk.

**5.** Add 1 cup of cranberry juice to 2 quarts of cooled tea. Garnish glasses with orange wheels.

**6.** Sweeten 2 quarts warm tea with ½ cup honey. Let cool. Add 1 cup apple juice and mix.

Love honey? Pair it with the simple accompaniments on page 108 and enjoy the whole comb ☞

## BLOODY MARY

The secret to a great Bloody Mary is to use tomato juice from whole tomatoes, not juice made from concentrate. This will give your cocktail an incredibly silken texture. It doesn't necessarily have to be fresh juice, but even puréeing a can of tomatoes is better than concentrate.

Treat your Bloody Mary like a cocktail rather than a salad. It's all about the balance of the vodka to the tomato juice and the texture of a few select ingredients. If you really want to ruin a Bloody Mary, overspice it, oversalt it, overgarnish it, and serve it in a pint glass over ice.

| | |
|---|---|
| 1 ½ ounces vodka | Juice of ½ lemon |
| 3 ounces tomato juice | Dash of salt |
| 2 dashes Worcestershire sauce | Freshly ground black pepper |

Shake all the ingredients with ice and strain into a small wine glass. Garnish with a lemon half-wheel and a twist of the pepper mill.

Note . . . Worcestershire and tomatoes are both inherently salty, so go easy when adding salt to the drink.

Victor Bergeron of Trader Vic's in San Francisco was the first bartender to stick cocktail umbrellas in drinks, but umbrellas have historically been a warning sign for things other than rampant tiki-dom.

FROM THE EPANACHE COLLECTIBLES GUIDE:

As the cocktail umbrella became a popular item, gang leaders in ghetto neighborhoods adopted the idea of placing them in their drinks as well as tucking them behind their ears, each using different colored umbrellas to state which gang they were affiliated with. This was particularly popular in the United States and spun off into gangs creating their own cocktail umbrellas to set themselves apart. The practice became less common after the mid 1960s, when . . . a regular toothpick was regarded as a more imposing object.

☞ Speculation attributes the invention of the bar to the famous Victorian engineer Isambard Kingdom Brunel, who created it to efficiently serve the sudden rush of customers disembarking from passenger trains.

SAZERAC

Created in New Orleans, the Sazerac gets its name from a number of sources, including the café where it was originally served (the Sazerac Coffee House) and the name of the rye whiskey that was originally used in the drink (Sazerac rye). The Sazerac Company continues to market the rye as well as Peychaud's bitters, an essential component of this drink. Like the Negroni, the Sazerac is an entirely grown-up beverage. This is a smoky, dark New Orleans jazz bar, not a deck in the Hamptons.

A few drops Herbsaint or pastis to coat glass
2 ounces rye whiskey

½ ounce simple syrup (recipe on page 25)
3 dashes Peychaud's bitters

Roll the Herbsaint around in a rocks glass to lightly coat the inside. Discard the excess. Combine rye, simple syrup, and bitters and shake with ice. Pour into the coated rocks glass.

For a coffee cocktail of a different sort, turn to page 49

"You're a rummy, but no more than most good writers are," were the all-too-true words uttered by Ernest Hemingway to F. Scott Fitzgerald. He and more than a handful of other infamous literary figures had their libations of choice.

**WILLIAM FAULKNER**......................................................Mint Julep

**F. SCOTT FITZGERALD**.......................................................Gin

**CHARLES BUKOWSKI**........................Boilermaker (surprised?)

**RAYMOND CARVER**.......................................................Bloody Mary

**JACK KEROUAC**..............................................................Margarita

**EUGENE O'NEILL**..........................................................Gin Gibson

**DYLAN THOMAS**................................................................Whiskey

**ALDOUS HUXLEY**.................................................................Wine

**TENNESSEE WILLIAMS**......................................Ramos Fizz

Like a good book to go with your cocktail? Turn to page 66 for some libation literature ☞

## JACK ROSE

One of our favorite classic cocktails, the Jack Rose, is favored
by one of our favorite customers: former San Francisco 49ers
quarterback Joe Montana. It's not often you walk into a bar and
order a round of Jack Roses. Jack is more of a solitary endeavor,
perfect for sipping. It may resemble a Cosmopolitan in hue, but
it's decidedly more interesting, apple-y, and tart. Applejack brandy
can be hard to find, but Calvados is an appropriate substitute.

1½ ounces applejack
  brandy
Juice of ½ lemon
1 ounce sweet-and-sour
  (recipe on page 25)

A drop of grenadine
  (as with the La Floridita
  Daiquiri, you want just a
  tiny amount)
1 teaspoon superfine sugar

Combine all ingredients and shake with ice. Strain into a martini glass. Garnish with a lemon wheel.

---

**Q:** All of the following personalities appeared in Smirnoff
ad campaigns in the 1960s except for:

A. Sean Connery
B. Woody Allen

c. Mae West
D. Bette Davis

See answer, page 156

When France banned absinthe in 1915, the ever-resourceful French simply took out the wormwood, a substance rumored to make absinthe drinkers hallucinate, go blind, and occasionally cut off ears. Thus pastis was born.

Pastis is commonly served in a collins glass over ice, with a carafe of water for the drinker to dilute the anise-flavored spirit to taste. Here are two less conventional ways to serve pastis:

## LA FEUILLE MORTE

The color of this traditional French drink is meant to resemble that of its namesake, a "dead leaf."

1½ ounces pastis ¾ ounce mint syrup
¾ ounce grenadine

Combine ingredients in a rocks glass with ice. Serve with ice water on the side.

## GOOD & PLENTY

A Doug "Bix" Biederbeck original.

1½ ounces pastis ||| 3 ounces freshly squeezed grapefruit juice

Combine ingredients in a highball glass with ice.

||||||||||||||||||||||||||||||||||||||||||||||||||||||||||||||||||||||||||||||||||||||||||||||||||||||||||||||||||||||||||||||||||||||||||||||||||||||||||||

MYTH: Pernod is pastis.

TRUTH: Pastis acquires its flavor from the maceration of aromatic ingredients in neutral alcohol. Pernod, unlike Ricard and many other French brands of pastis, is a distillate made from a wine flavored with anise, fennel, and other herbs.

## MARTINI

If you thought you could finish this book without learning how to make a genuine, honest-to-God Martini, you are indeed mistaken. We have a few tips to help make your creation perfect. As taste in gin is intensely personal, we won't recommend a particular brand. However, you might note the proof of various gins (see below) and decide which one agrees with you.

2 ounces dry gin  ||| ¼ ounce dry vermouth

Shake ingredients with ice in a cocktail shaker and strain into a chilled martini glass. Garnish with olives, onions, or a lemon twist.

### PROOFS OF A FEW WELL-KNOWN GINS

| | |
|---|---|
| TANQUERAY | 94.6 |
| TANQUERAY No. TEN | 94.6 |
| BEEFEATER | 94 |
| BOMBAY | 86 |
| BOMBAY SAPPHIRE | 94 |
| PLYMOUTH | 82.4 |
| HENDRICK'S | 88 |
| BOODLES | 90.4 |

**1.** Vermouth is a fortified wine. Store it in the refrigerator, tightly sealed, and it will keep from oxidizing for several months.

If you're out of vermouth, you can substitute fino sherry. See page 39 page 39 ▀◣

**2.** Though everyone seems to think Martinis should be bone-dry, they were not invented that way. Bix makes a fairly wet one.

**3.** Use a metal shaker, which is a better conductor of temperature than a glass or plastic one. We like our Martinis to be as cold as possible.

**4.** We are deeply troubled by birdbath-sized cocktail glasses. Martinis must be consumed at Arctic temperatures, and unless you gulp it, a 6- or 7-ounce Martini is bound to be warm by the time you finish. Order a second drink instead.

For a quick glimpse at some proper barware, turn to page 20 ▀◣

A DRINK WITH SOMETHING IN IT

There is something about a Martini,
A tingle remarkably pleasant;
A yellow, a mellow Martini;
I wish I had one at present.
There is something about a Martini,
Ere the dining and dancing begin,
And to tell you the truth,
It is not the vermouth—
I think that perhaps it's the gin.

☛ OGDEN NASH

I like to have a Martini, two at the very most; three, I'm under the table, four I'm under my host!

☛ DOROTHY PARKER

One Martini is all right.
Two are too many, and three are not enough.

☛ JAMES THURBER

One of the men we credit as the "conscience" of our bar is Tim Savinar, whom we have to thank for helping us track down Gran Torres, an orange liqueur similar to Grand Marnier. Made in Spain, Gran Torres is a brandy-based spirit in which the rinds of Valencia oranges have been macerated. It is slightly more aromatic and heavier than other orange liqueurs, which often serve to sweeten drinks but don't offer any complexity of flavor.

### GRAN TORRES MARGARITA

Juice of ½ lime
½ ounce simple syrup
(recipe on page 25)

1½ ounce tequila
Splash of Gran Torres

Combine all ingredients over ice and gently shake or stir.

Note . . . A quick note on salted rims: Salt originally appeared on tequila drinks as a means of hiding the taste of horrid, cheap booze, much in the same way vermouth was added to Martinis to mellow the shocking undrinkability of bathtub gin. The salt garnish has since become a standard on most American preparations of the Margarita. Ditch it. Instead, experiment with *reposado* or *añejo* tequilas, and savor your drink.

# CLEVER RHYMES
# AND COMPLEX FORMS

**IF THE TRUTH WERE KNOWN ABOUT THE ORIGIN OF THE WORD
"JAZZ" IT WOULD NEVER BE MENTIONED IN POLITE SOCIETY.**

☛ CLAY SMITH, *ETUDE* MAGAZINE, SEPTEMBER 1924

One of the earliest-known references to the word "jazz" is found in a *Los Angeles Times* article dated April 2, 1912. Oddly enough, it has nothing to do with music, but rather, Ben Henderson's new pitch for the Portland Beavers: "'I got a new curve this year,' softly murmured Henderson yesterday, 'and I'm goin' to pitch one or two of them tomorrow. I call it the Jazz ball because it wobbles and you simply can't do anything with it.'"

Sadly, Mr. Henderson's "Jazz ball" was hardly a success, but the term "jazz" has been with us ever since. The embodiment of youth and energy, jazz can somehow stamp any occasion with its particular brand of sophistication and recklessness. At Bix we are lucky to have had so many talented musicians develop our musical identity. The lineup is always changing, the sound is always fresh, and the music is always free of charge. Everyone knows a little something about jazz, and everyone has his or her favorite numbers. In this book, we decided to list our own.

But even if Bix is all about the music, it's not *only* about the music, just as while putting food on the table certainly lies at the heart of what we do, the physical act of eating does not make a meal. A great dinner is made up of many things: food, friends, perhaps one more glass of wine, and ideally someone to foot the bill.

We also thought we'd share a list of some of our favorite food literature. As in any literary genre, there are books you have to read, and then there are books you *get* to read. All of our picks reflect our own highly selective, personal criteria for essential entertainment: lively, spirited, authentic, and truly inspired by the subject matter. Any one of these books makes a great gift, and all are sure to spark conversation at your next dinner party.

Not satisfied with the "Jazz ball" either? Turn to page 86 for more speculation on the origin of the word ☞

Nearly all the art in Bix Restaurant came from Modernism, a San Francisco gallery owned by our great friend and patron, Martin Muller, who is a fastidious Swiss intellectual and a connoisseur of fine food and drink. It is only with his help that we have been able to assemble the paintings now in our collection.

The most prominent piece is *The Butler's in Love—Absinthe* by Oakland artist Mark Stock. Painted in haste for a black-tie celebration at Bix, it was intended to be displayed only temporarily. Twenty years later, the painting is still hanging over the piano, the centerpiece of the entire restaurant.

Other paintings include Mindy Lehrman's mural over our bar, commissioned for the restaurant. The mural was intentionally painted to appear "unfinished," to act as a reflection or mirror image of the restaurant. Upstairs in the mezzanine, the painting of the woman clothed in only a giant tuba is by Constantine Titov. The mysterious, dark paintings upstairs of Billy Holiday and Charlie Parker are by Gottfried Helnwein.

We have several vintage 1920s prints of the Bal Nègre and a small cabinet, tucked away on the mezzanine, that holds rare books, liqueurs, and cocktail shakers. In a shadow box on the second floor is a plate from an edition of ceramics done by Picasso. Roughly 50 percent of our guests also get to enjoy the vintage illustration *The Isle of Pleasure* by H. J. Lawrence, which is hung lovingly over the men's urinal.

## ADVENTURES ON THE WINE ROUTE:
## A WINE BUYER'S TOUR OF FRANCE

BY KERMIT LYNCH

Wine importer Kermit Lynch has a legendary palate. His taste is impeccable, yet his writing never overcomplicates the pleasure of drinking wine. If you know nothing about France or wine in general, you will enjoy following Lynch as he describes his journey through the provinces. Opinionated and personal, he is so direct in his enjoyment of wine that you're reminded of the simple pleasure that comes with new discoveries:

Rhône wine, we say, but it is badly said, because a Rhône wine can be red, white, or pink, sweet or dry, still or sparkling. It can be from one grape variety or a blend of several. It can be among the handful of France's noblest wines, or it can be a simple wine whose proper place would be in a carafe alongside a quick steak and french fries.

Sipping have you tongue-tied? Spit it out with a few of the quick fixes on page 47 🖘

**THE MARTINI:**

**AN ILLUSTRATED HISTORY OF AN AMERICAN CLASSIC**

BY BARNABY CONRAD III

Author of six books, dear friend, and patron of the restaurant, Conrad delves into the complex history of this iconic drink. The exhaustive amount of work that went into the preparation of the book is evident—we should know, since we spent several late nights helping with his "research." *The Martini* is lively and intelligently presented, and the graphic nature of its contents offers not just a thorough history of the drink but a visually arresting read. Art, history, recipes, lore, and even scientific formulas are included in this extensive portrait. From the chapter "The Social Career of a Drink":

Until Prohibition ended in 1934, Americans had little access to high-proof, highly fragrant gins, but the cheap stuff was easy to make. "The gin is aged about the length of time it takes to get from the bathroom where it is made to the front porch where the cocktail party is in progress," claimed one bar book. So bartenders disguised bathtub gin with a "civilizing" dose of vermouth in a one-to-two ratio.

## THE FABER BOOK OF DRINK, DRINKERS, AND DRINKING

### EDITED BY SIMON RAE

Gathering together everyone from George Orwell to Ezra Pound, Thomas Pynchon to Dylan Thomas, *Drink, Drinkers, and Drinking* is a compendium of literature about every imaginable aspect of the culture of drinking. Its information is organized into subheadings such as "Philosophies," "Effects," "Trouble," "Pro and Con," and "Admonitions," so you're sure to find exactly what you're looking for. From the editor's introduction:

When I began thinking about this anthology some three years ago, I drew up a list of names and titles which convinced me there would be sufficient material. As I actually started reading for the book, I realized there was enough for any number of anthologies. Once you start looking, drink, drinkers, and drinking crop up in the most astonishing variety of places, and this selection can have no claims to be definitive.

It was not uncommon in times past for artists to trade their skills for supper and a warm bed. Restaurants remain dedicated homes to notable art collections:

☞ The Pied Piper Bar, in San Francisco's Palace Hotel, is home to Maxfield Parrish's mural *The Pied Piper of Hamlin*, which was commissioned for the reopening of the structure after the Great San Francisco Earthquake of 1906.

☞ The Palace was not the only hotel bar to house a Parrish painting. John Jacob Astor commissioned *Old King Cole*, also in 1906, and today it hangs behind the bar at the St. Regis Hotel in New York. A January 17, 2007, *New York Times* article revealed the truth behind the smirk on the old king's face: "Through decades of mixed-drink conviviality, bartenders have shared with their regulars a secret of the painting that is considerably less elegant than the hotel, the bar, or indeed the mural itself. The legend, repeated by generations of bar patrons, is that the king's sheepish grin, and the startled reactions of his knights, were occasioned by the flatulence of the monarch."

☞ At Kronenhalle, a Zurich restaurant, you can dine in the "Swiss Gallery," a room dedicated to the oil paintings of Segatini, Hodler, and Giacometti.

☞ Named for the artist and children's book author Ludwig Bemelmans, Bemelmans Bar in New York's Carlyle Hotel houses the only artwork by the artist still available for public viewing.

☞ La Columbe d'Or in St. Paul de Vence, France, houses perhaps the most noteworthy art collection of any private restaurant in the world. There are Matisses, Mirós, and perhaps $100 million worth of art scattered about this incredibly elegant restaurant.

☞ La Grenouille, on East 52nd Street in New York, has been dazzling guests with its breathtaking décor since it first opened its doors in 1962. The artistic attraction is not art in the classic sense, but rather its stunning floral arrangements and ceiling-high bouquets.

MYTH: Vodka is distilled from potatoes

TRUTH: Vodka is made from a variety of materials. What gives vodka its neutral flavor—regardless of whether it is made from grain, potatoes, molasses, or otherwise—is endless distillation. Tinkering with the infinite variables in the process is what gives different brands of vodka their defining characteristics. Two of the most widely available potato vodkas are Chopin and Luksusowa.

## THE RAW AND THE COOKED:
## ADVENTURES OF A ROVING GOURMAND

BY JIM HARRISON

A gifted writer, poet, and culinary hedonist, Harrison has written many famous works of fiction, including *Dalva*, *Julip*, *A Good Day to Die*, and *Legends of the Fall*. He's also published a mountain of poetry and two works of nonfiction, including *The Raw and the Cooked*. Completely endearing and accessible, this collection of essays chronicles Harrison's adventures with food—raw, cooked, or otherwise. From "Thirty-three Angles on Eating French":

> Even dogs love good food. Rub a piece of steak with garlic, fry it in butter, and give it to your pooch. The dog will say clearly, "This beats the shit out of kibble."

Dr. Seuss created *Green Eggs and Ham* after his editor dared him to write a book using fewer than fifty different words. Turn to page 88 for another little-known fact ☞

## THE ART OF EATING

BY M. F. K. FISHER

*The Art of Eating* is a collection of five books, originally published separately. If any food book can be defined as a "classic," this is it. Fisher's knowledge of food is exhaustive, and her authoritative writing style has inspired thousands of people in the food business. Here she discusses steak tartare:

> This somewhat barbaric dish is best with crisp bread and a glass of fairly plain red wine. It is quickly digested and leaves a pleasant feeling on the palate, if you can swallow it at all, which some people would rather starve than do . . .

Feeling uncivilized? To learn more about steak tartare, turn to page 120 ☞

## LIFE IS MEALS:
## A FOOD LOVER'S BOOK OF DAYS

BY JAMES AND KAY SALTER

*Life Is Meals* is composed of 365 entries encompassing entertaining, drinking, and eating. Terribly sophisticated, very personal, and infused with a sense of pleasure, this book makes you wish the authors would invite you over:

Waiters are one thing, a face-to-face matter: Room service is another. You are on the phone talking to someone unseen and located who-knows-exactly-where.

Irving Lazar, better known as Swifty . . . once was staying in at a hotel in the American West and in the morning called down to order breakfast . . .

He wanted toast, he said, burned on one side but untoasted on the other. He would also like a soft-boiled egg, he continued, but not completely cooked, mucous-y on top. And coffee—not hot, however, just tepid. How long would that take? "I'm sorry, sir," was the answer, "but we're not equipped to do that." "You were yesterday," Lazar replied dryly.

## THE MAN WHO ATE EVERYTHING

BY JEFFREY STEINGARTEN

This noted food columnist's very male-centric point of view goes a long way toward explaining your man's inexplicable stash of *Vogue* magazines. *The Man Who Ate Everything* is a collection of his painstakingly detailed adventures in the kitchen. The second essay, "Staying Alive," opens thus:

> Years ago I read somewhere that the absolutely cheapest survival diet consists of peanut butter, whole wheat bread, nonfat dry milk, and a vitamin pill. Eager to try it, I rushed to the supermarket, returned home with provisions for a week's survival, and went to work with my calculator and butter knife.

For a decidedly more palatable survival diet, try your hand at a croque, page 116 ☞

## THE GENTLEMAN'S COMPANION

BY CHARLES H. BAKER JR.

Extra credit if you can track this book down, because it's out of print. The subtitle to the first volume is *Including: A company of hand-picked Receipts, each one Beloved & Notable in its Place, collected faithfully on Three Voyages & a Quarter Million Miles around the World, & other Journeys.* A recipe from the book speaks to the author's considerable charm:

The Cajuns are strange people, a blend of Portuguese, Indian, and heaven only knows what else. They fish, shrimp, trap fur in the maze of bayous and marshes of the big Delta. Priests wade into the water and bless their shrimp boats at start of season. They know how to cook turtles. Our only recommended addition is a can of chopped button mushrooms. Trim 2 lbs turtle steak into 1½" squares, season well with salt and hand-ground black pepper, squeeze on some lemon or sour orange juice, and stand a while. Add plenty of chopped onion, a sweet pepper chopped well, 3 or 4 tomatoes cut into eights, 3 bay leaves, a crushed garlic clove, and mushrooms . . . Serve with big mounds of rice. This will nourish 4 hungry folk.

**COD:**
**A BIOGRAPHY OF THE FISH THAT CHANGED THE WORLD**

BY MARK KURLANSKY

Every serious food nut has read this book, though it's not about eating per se but the origin of a specific food. Who would've thought the history of a single fish could be so fascinating? Well researched and highly readable, the book also packs a punch: It's shocking to eventually realize that this once-plentiful food source is now in danger of extinction. Kurlansky has given the same historical treatment to two other foods in his books *The Big Oyster: History on a Half Shell* and *Salt: A World History.* From *Cod:*

A medieval fisherman is said to have hauled up a three-foot-long cod, which was common enough at the time. And the fact that the cod could talk was not especially surprising. But what *was* astonishing was that is spoke an unknown language. It spoke Basque.

Those looking for a more hands-on experience can try shucking their own oysters by following the simple instructions on page 137 ☛

## KITCHEN CONFIDENTIAL:
## ADVENTURES IN THE CULINARY UNDERBELLY

BY ANTHONY BOURDAIN

The appeal of *Kitchen Confidential*—a book whose acknowledgments page thanks the author's "ass-kicking crew in the kitchen"—lies not only in Bourdain's recklessness but also his ability to describe the manic pace of restaurant life. His take on those who choose to inhabit this lifestyle is completely accurate:

> The most dangerous species of owner . . . a true menace to himself and others . . . is the one that gets into the business for love.

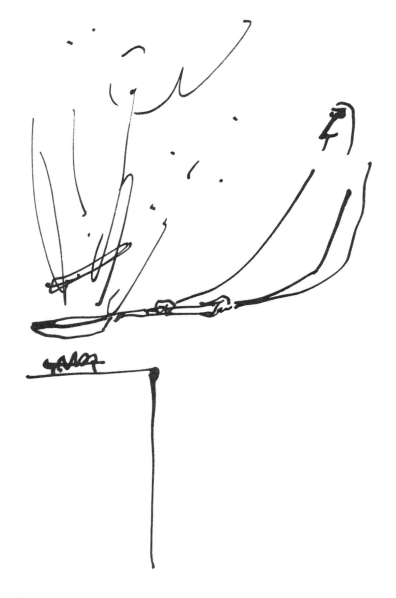

## AMERICAN FRIED: ADVENTURES OF A HAPPY EATER
### BY CALVIN TRILLIN

Trillin, one of our cherished friends, has been writing for the *New Yorker* since 1963. He has also contributed to the *Nation*, specifically a column titled "Uncivil Liberties." Trillin's knack for irony isn't evident only in his clever titles, but is immediately apparent in his prose as well:

> The best restaurants in the world are, of course, in Kansas City. Not all of them; only the top four or five . . . I know the problem of asking someone in a strange city for the best restaurant in town and being led to some purple palace that serves "continental cuisine" . . . I have sat in those places, an innocent wayfarer, reading a three-paragraph description of what the trout is wrapped in, how long it has been sautéed, what province its sauce comes from, and what it is likely to sound like sizzling on my platter—a description lacking only the information that before the poor beast went through that process it had been frozen for eight and a half months.

## THE OMNIVORE'S DILEMMA:
## A NATURAL HISTORY OF FOUR MEALS

BY MICHAEL POLLAN

The omnivore's dilemma: What should you eat if you can eat basically anything? The reader's dilemma: Do I really want to snooze through another book from a Berkeley academic? *The Omnivore's Dilemma* is decidedly the most serious book on our list, and perhaps the most widely known as well, but it would be a mistake to pass it over because of its renown. The book's intelligent reflections on our culture could only have been written by someone who truly loved food:

Air-conditioned, odorless, illuminated by buzzing fluorescent tubes, the American supermarket doesn't present itself as having very much to do with Nature. And yet what is this place if not a landscape (man-made, it's true) teeming with plants and animals?

The strawberry-lover's dilemma: choosing between the tasty recipes on page 150 ☞

## BETWEEN MEALS:
## AN APPETITE FOR PARIS

BY A. J. LIEBLING

This period piece by *New Yorker* staff writer Liebling conjures up the joy and intensity of French cooking in 1926 and 1927 and a custom the author refers to as the fine art of "feeding." In his introduction, James Salter describes Liebling as "belong[ing] to the generation, now gone, that lived through both World Wars and, further, to that fabled splinter of that new Paris in what seems to us its most glorious days."

If, as I was saying before I digressed, the first requisite for writing well about food is a good appetite, the second is to put in your apprenticeship as feeder when you have enough money to pay the check but not enough to produce indifference to the size of the total.

## AND ALL THAT JAZZ

Where did the word *jazz* come from? No one is sure.
Three possibilities:

**1.** It was first recorded in the lyrics of a 1909 song, "Uncle
Josh in Society" ("One lady asked me if I danced the jazz . . ."),
where it apparently refers to a style of ragtime dancing.

**2.** *Jazz* originated from a twist on the band name "Razzy
Dazzy Spasm Band," comprised of seven boys who performed
in New Orleans in late 1895.

**3.** According to Alyn Shipton's *A New History of Jazz*, the
word *jazz* or *jass* was shouted in a derogatory fashion at a
white jazz band in 1915. Shipton laims it was "a scatological
term for sexual congress that seems to have its origins in
the San Francisco area, where the word also meant 'pep' or
'enthusiasm.'"

Mesmerized by mystery? Visit the enigmatic Lady Day on page 97
for another dose of irresistible mystique ☞

American folklore attributes certain unsavory supernatural forces not only to the excesses of food and drink, but to many other artistic enterprises as well:

☞ Legend has it that famous blues musician Robert Johnson achieved mastery of the guitar by selling his soul to the devil late one night at a plantation crossroads in Mississippi.

☞ "The Devil and Tom Walker" is a short story by Washington Irving in which the protagonist sells his soul to become wealthy.

☞ Stephen Vincent Benét's short story "The Devil and Daniel Webster" pits famed orator Daniel Webster against the devil in court.

☞ Italian violin player Niccolò Paganini's technique was so difficult to reproduce that a legend arose that his ability was the product of a pact with the devil. Later speculation attributes it to Marfan's syndrome, a connective-tissue disorder that makes fingers elongated and joints abnormally flexible.

☞ The term "devil's bridge" has been given to a few dozen ancient bridges with masterful craftsmanship. According to folklore, the builder of the bridge either bested the devil in a contest or promised Satan that he would receive the first soul who crossed the bridge once it was completed.

**LOTHARIO:** A man who obsessively seduces and deceives women

**ORIGIN:** A character in Nicholas Rowe's 1703 play *The Fair Penitent*, Lothario seduces and then betrays the female protagonist.

**LILLIPUTIAN:** Diminutive in size, small

**ORIGIN:** Lilliput (as well as Blefuscu, its minuscule neighbor) is a fictional island nation populated by tiny people in *Gulliver's Travels* by Jonathan Swift.

**NERD:** An intelligent person obsessed with a nonsocial pursuit

**ORIGIN:** The first known appearance of the word *nerd* in print is in Dr. Seuss's 1950 children's book, *If I Ran the Zoo:*

> The whole town will gasp, "Why, this boy never sleeps!
> No keeper before ever kept what *he* keeps!
> There's no telling WHAT that young fellow will do!"
> And then, just to show them, I'll sail to Ka-Troo
> And bring back an IT-KUTCH a PREEP and a PROO
> A NERKLE a NERD and a SEERSUCKER, too!

**PANGLOSSIAN**: Characterized by or given to extreme optimism, especially in the face of unrelieved hardship

**ORIGIN**: Dr. Pangloss, a character in Voltaire's *Candide*, is fond of repeating, "All is for the best in the best of all possible worlds."

**IGNORAMUS**: An utterly ignorant person, a dunce

**ORIGIN**: George Ruggle titled his 1615 play, a satire of the legal profession, *Ignoramus*.

☞ L. Frank Baum named "Oz" after a file cabinet in his office. One cabinet was labeled "A to N," and the second was labeled "O to Z."

## MILES DAVIS

### KIND OF BLUE, 1959

*Kind of Blue* is universally recognized as the jazz standard of excellence, so why bother mentioning it? Perhaps it has more to do with Davis than the album. He was not a follower of jazz—jazz followed him. He employed every new technique, he was at the forefront of every innovation, he carefully selected the best of his contemporaries to be his collaborators. *Birth of the Cool* gave birth to the cool jazz movement and came to define Davis's mellow, relaxed style. But Davis never worried about sticking to a genre. In fact, he is the only jazz musician so far to be inducted into the Rock and Roll Hall of Fame. *Kind of Blue* is unique in Davis's catalogue of more than one hundred albums because it represents a once-in-a-lifetime level of collaboration and communication between Davis and his musicians. Conditions were perfect, and in that exact moment, everyone involved in the recording was no longer playing for themselves but striving for the same sound, the same tone, the same level of perfection.

We play what the day recommends.

☞ MILES DAVIS

## HERBIE HANCOCK

MAIDEN VOYAGE, 1965

Just like Miles Davis, Hancock drove purists mad. A piano prodigy at twelve, Hancock embraced all manner of electronic devices later in life, including synthesizers, effects pedals, the Rhodes piano, Clavinets, and computers. He often bordered on the avant-garde and even suffered an unfortunate stumble into disco. *Maiden Voyage*, a concept album, is centered around five tracks with ocean themes. It was recorded early in his career while he was playing in Miles Davis's band. Hancock recently won his eleventh Grammy for a Joni Mitchell covers album titled *River: The Joni Letters*.

The 33⅓ rpm "long-playing" microgroove record was introduced in 1948. It could hold twenty-five minutes of music per side, as opposed to the paltry four minutes per side of its predecessor, the 78 rpm.

**CHARLIE PARKER, DIZZY GILLESPIE,
BUD POWELL, MAX ROACH, AND CHARLES MINGUS,
A.K.A. "THE QUINTET"**

JAZZ AT MASSEY HALL, 1953

With Parker playing a borrowed plastic alto saxophone, Gillespie on trumpet, Powell on piano, Roach on percussion, and Mingus on the bass, this recording brought together five of the heaviest hitters in bebop history and resulted in jazz brilliance. In an effort to skirt contractual obligations, Parker is listed on the album as "Charlie Chan." It is said that the audience at this concert was so small that the Toronto New Jazz Society, with whom the players were to split the profits, was unable to pay the musicians for the performance.

Trying to create that jazz club vibe in your own home? Page 55 has a recipe for the perfect drink 👉

## ART BLAKEY

THE JAZZ MESSENGERS AT THE CAFE BOHEMIA, VOL. I, 1955

Blue Note Records, founded in 1939, is in certain terms the most successful and influential recording studio of all time, home to more legendary musicians in a specific genre than any other studio to date. The Jazz Messengers' first recording is potentially the album that solidified Blue Note's status. Blakey was a jazz drummer, the guiding force behind the Jazz Messengers. In hindsight, the Messengers were not just a band, but almost a master class through which the greatest jazz players of the century began refining and learning the true depth of their talent, before moving onto solo careers. Blakey was an incubator of jazz talent for more than thirty years.

BLUE NOTE: A note in blues played a pitch lower than the note on the traditional major scale.

BROWN NOTE: The brown note, according to an urban legend, is an infrasound frequency whose resonance causes humans to lose control of their bowels.

## BILL EVANS TRIO

WALTZ FOR DEBBY, 1961

All of the jazz greats had their trademark sound, and pianist Bill Evans is no exception. His sensibilities led him to harmonic sounds and classic European song structures. He leans so dramatically in that direction that he was once accused of not being able to swing. (Obviously untrue.) Evans was Miles Davis's piano player on *Kind of Blue*, and Davis wrote in his autobiography, "Bill had this quiet fire that I loved on piano. The way he approached it, the sound he got was like crystal notes or sparkling water cascading down from some clear waterfall." Released on the heels of *Kind of Blue*, *Waltz for Debby* was a highlight of the pianist's already impressive career and contains some of his most recognizable melodies. Debby is Evans's niece.

## BOB DOROUGH

### SONGS OF LOVE, (IMPORT) 1987

Dorough was the main composer and singer for *Schoolhouse Rock!* a popular series of children's television spots that aired in the 1970s and 1980s. He has also collaborated with several personalities outside the jazz circle, including Allen Ginsberg, Sugar Ray Robinson, and Lenny Bruce. A skinny white guy who sings at the piano, Dorough is still the ultimate hipster. We adore his rendition of "Down in the Depths (on the Ninetieth Floor)," a Cole Porter song.

## BILLIE HOLIDAY

### LADY IN SATIN, 1958

Billie Holiday made pop vocals what they are today. She was one of the first performers to take on the work of making you believe that she had lived and felt what she was singing. In an era of interchangeable singers, she was irreplaceable. Holiday led a tragic life that to this day remains clouded by legend and myth, and died of liver and heart disease at the age of forty-four. This was one of her final albums, and her vocals make the weight of her entire life palpable.

## BLOSSOM DEARIE

BALLADS, (VERVE JAZZ MASTERS 51)

Anyone who has ever heard Blossom Dearie's little-girl voice will never forget it (and that *is* her real name). Yet despite her vocal timbre, her phrasing remains powerful, precise, and clear. She has performed in supper clubs most of her life, and later in her career formed her own label, Daffodil Records, in order to have more creative control over her songs. This album is a collection of jazz and pop standards, with both piano and vocals by Dearie; for the uninitiated listener, it is a great starting point for getting to know her body of work.

## BILL EVANS AND TONY BENNETT

THE TONY BENNETT/BILL EVANS ALBUM, 1975

This album represented a unique moment in the vocal superstar's recording career, when he was no longer signed to any label and hadn't been working. Not only that, Evans rarely accompanied vocalists on piano. There was utterly no indication that their collaboration would work, and yet the two musicians produced one of the few true jazz vocal classics, which matches the clear precision and elegant dexterity of Evans's piano playing with Bennett's pristine phrasing and trademark tenor.

## SARAH VAUGHAN

LIVE IN JAPAN, 1973

Vaughan's strength was not in recording but in live performance. "I can't sing a blues—just a right-out blues," she once told *Down Beat* magazine, "but I can put the blues in whatever I sing." Her appetite for nightlife was legendary, and after performances she regularly stayed out partying well into the next day. *Live in Japan* was recorded later in Vaughan's life, before a hugely appreciative audience. Even in the twilight years of her career, her vocal range failed to diminish. It was often said that she could have been an opera singer.

One thing I like about jazz, kid, is that I don't know what's going to happen next. Do you?

☞ BIX BEIDERBECKE

Sometimes classic means "timeless," and sometimes it just means old. Here are three true musical classics:

**DIDGERIDOO:** The Australian didgeridoo is believed to be more than fifteen hundred years old, judging by dates on indigenous cave art depicting its use.

**BONES:** Made from the ribs of goats or sheep, bones are rivaled only by sticks, rocks, clapping hands, and stomping feet as the oldest instrument. Egyptian frescoes depicting "clapping" type artifacts date as far back as the fourth century B.C.E.

**BIRD FLUTES:** Chinese scholars have recovered six bone flutes dating from eight thousand to nine thousand years ago. Crafted from the hollow wing bones of red-crowned cranes, the flutes are the world's oldest playable, multinote instruments.

Need an ancient recipe to pair with these classics? Turn to page 118 for the perfect accompaniment from ancient Rome ☛

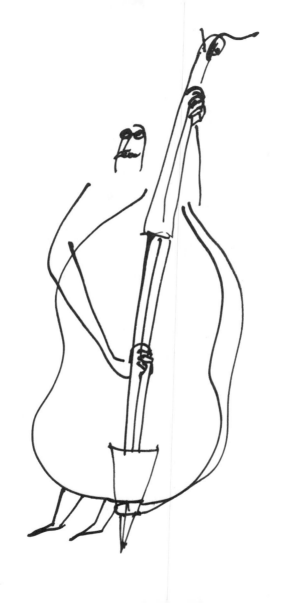

Here are ten essential albums no jazz lover worthy of the title should be without:

**ERROLL GARNER**......................................................*Concert by the Sea*
**THE MODERN JAZZ QUARTET**...........................................*Django*
**THE DAVE BRUBECK QUARTET**.................................*Time Out*
**CLIFFORD BROWN AND MAX ROACH**...................*Study in Brown*
**CANNONBALL ADDERLEY**.................................*Somethin' Else*
**ELLA FITZGERALD AND LOUIS ARMSTRONG**.......*Ella and Louis*
**DINAH WASHINGTON**.........................*The Swingin' Miss 'D'*
**CHARLIE PARKER**.................*Quasimodo: The Dial Sessions*
**BUD POWELL**.......................................*The Scene Changes*
**BIX BEIDERBECKE**.............................*Singin' the Blues* (after all . . . )

How dare we leave out:

**DAVE FRISHBERG**...........................*Can't Take You Nowhere*
**FRANK SINATRA**.................................*In the Wee Small Hours*
**MABEL MERCER**...........................*Midnight at Mabel Mercer's*

No self-respecting jazz legend goes by his given name. Here are the pseudonyms of ten greats:

**LEADBELLY**.................................................Huddie Ledbetter

**SATCHMO**....................................................Louie Armstrong

**COUNT BASIE**...............................................William Basie

**JELLY ROLL MORTON**...................................Ferdinand La Menthe

**DIZZY GILLESPIE**..........................................John Gillespie

**DJANGO REINHARDT**...................................Jean-Baptiste Reinhardt

**CANNONBALL ADDERLEY**............................Julian Adderley

**SONNY ROLLINS**...........................................Theodore Rollins

**Q:** What was McKinley Morganfield's famous stage name?

A. Fats Walker           c. Muddy Waters
B. Boots Morgan          D. Buddy Maynard

See answer, page 156

# SIMPLE PLEASURES

**I NEVER EAT IN A RESTAURANT THAT'S OVER ONE HUNDRED FEET OFF THE GROUND AND WON'T STAND STILL.**

☞ CALVIN TRILLIN

As a host, it's important to keep in mind a healthy bit of reality: Your visitors are not trekking all the way across town to see you. They're coming for the food.

Few things are more special than a big night out at a great restaurant where a talented chef combines flavors and textures in surprising, unimaginable ways. And certain holidays are absolutely defined by an all-day, labor-intensive orchestration of stuffing, roasting, and carving.

But not every occasion benefits from such daunting effort, and no host should be stuck in the kitchen at his or her own get-together. So we have included a few great ideas for party foods, the kind of simple fare that, when prepared with a special ingredient or presented in an interesting way, can transform an offhand gathering into something memorable.

We have found that starters on our menu are some of its main attractions. Why not make a meal of them? Start with some Champagne Cocktails (page 30). Pass some Mini Burgers (page 133). And enjoy your party.

You can pile food on a plate in any manner you wish, but there are a few tried-and-true ways to present your culinary efforts:

**STACKED:** one ingredient on top of the other, a popular restaurant style

**DECONSTRUCTED:** all of the ingredients together on a plate, but uncombined and meant to be enjoyed separately

**TRADITIONAL:** starch at ten o'clock, vegetables at two, the entrée straddling four to eight

---

### THREE WAYS TO EAT HONEYCOMB

1. With crackers and blue cheese

2. With peanut butter and apples on toast

3. Drizzled with melted dark chocolate

**Q:** How did the cantaloupe get its name?

A. From the names of the ships that first exported the melon out of Europe to the southern Mediterranean

B. From Gianni Canta, a turn-of-the-century Italian baker

C. From *canton*, the French word for "district"

D. From Cantalupo, the Italian estate where the melons were first grown

See answer, page 156

Nutty for nomenclature? Turn to page 105 to learn the real names behind some famous monikers

## BRUSCHETTA with AVOCADO, WHITE ANCHOVIES, and GREEN ONIONS

Bruschetta is Italian garlic bread. That's it! The most popular American version is topped with olive oil, basil, and tomatoes, but it's not the tomato that makes the appetizer. In Italian, *bruscare* means "to roast over coals," so it's the toasting that defines the dish. The traditional recipe has you drizzle your bread with a little olive oil, and salt and pepper the bread to taste before tossing it in the oven. When it comes out of the oven, rub it with garlic. The tradition started when Italian farmers processed their olives at the end of the growing season. They'd take a loaf of bread along, toast it in the fireplace—it was early winter, after all—and use the bread to sample the oil as it came out of the press.

Who says six centuries of tradition can't be improved upon? You can top your bruschetta however you like. One of our favorite recipes adds a distinctly Californian twist: avocado.

1 loaf Italian country bread, sliced ⅜" thick

2 to 3 fresh cloves of garlic

1 avocado, peeled, pitted, and sliced as thinly as a possible (or, honestly, mashed if slicing isn't your thing)

Maldon salt

12 anchovy fillets (see Note)

2 tablespoons red wine vinaigrette

1 bunch scallions, finely sliced

Preheat the oven to 350°F. Brush the bread with oil. Place bread on the baking sheet and toast for 5 to 8 minutes, or until golden brown. Remove from oven and rub lightly with garlic. You can also grill the bread for a better result. Fan or spread your avocado on the toast. Season with a pinch of salt. Lay an anchovy over the avocado. Brush with red wine vinaigrette, and sprinkle with scallions.

Note . . . Look for oil-packed white anchovies, known as *boquerones* in Spain; slightly pickled, they have less salt and more flavor—definitely worth it!

How about a Bloody with your bruschetta? Turn to page 51

## DUNGENESS CRAB ROLLS
## with MEYER LEMON MAYONNAISE

This recipe should be modified to showcase the ingredients you
have available locally. Dungeness crabs live in the Pacific and
inhabit the waters from central California up through the Aleu-
tian Islands in Alaska. The most available variety of Atlantic
Ocean crab is the blue crab. Unlike with crab cakes, you don't
need to add anything to stick the crab together into a patty—
you're just going to enhance the crab's delicate flavor and leave
the texture intact.

**TO MAKE THE MAYONNAISE:**

2 egg yolks

Zest of two Meyer lemons,
grated or minced to a
powder

¼ cup plus 2 teaspoons
Meyer lemon juice

2 drops Sriracha or other
hot-pepper sauce

1½ cups olive oil

Salt and pepper

Combine the yolks, zest, juice, and Sriracha together in a food
processor, and blend until frothy. Slowly add olive oil—starting
with a few drops at a time, eventually in a thin stream—until all
ingredients are combined. Season to taste with salt and pepper.

**TO MAKE THE ROLLS:**

1 loaf brioche bread
measuring 3½ x 3½ x 15"

4 tablespoons butter

First, cut the crusts off your bread. Then slice the entire loaf lengthwise, then cut each half lengthwise again to yield four bread "batons" of equal size. Ideally, you want a 7-inch-long piece of brioche whose width and height are both 1½ inches, so trim accordingly. Cut a small portion, lengthwise, out of the middle of each baton so you have a U-shaped hollow to nestle the crab in. Brush each piece of brioche with butter and toast on all sides, preferably on a a griddle, until all sides are golden brown.

**TO MAKE THE CRAB ROLL:**

12 ounces lump crab meat (If you're already springing for fresh crab, save yourself the work of cleaning the beasts. Seriously.)

1 to 1½ cups Meyer Lemon Mayonnaise

½ cup celery, brunoise (inner stalks are sweeter)

1 tablespoon finely chopped fresh chives plus more for garnish

Salt and pepper

Brioche rolls

In a mixing bowl, combine the crab with enough mayonnaise to form a moist mixture. Add the celery and chives, and mix all ingredients until combined. Season to taste with salt and pepper.

Fill the brioche batons with the crab mixture, then slice each long baton into bite-size pieces. Garnish with chives.

Looking for a little additional maritime inspiration? Try the album on page 91 🔊

## FRESH BEETS and GOAT CHEESE

As easy as serving celery or carrots, fresh beets add exceptionally bright colors and fresh flavors to any ordinary plate of crudités. If you have hesitant beet lovers in your midst, win them over with this simple preparation of beets, goat cheese, basil, aged balsamic vinegar, and olive oil.

Cube one medium roasted, peeled beet (red, gold, chiogga—any type will do). Place the cubes on a plate and season with sea salt. Crumble 2 to 3 ounces of goat cheese atop the beet cubes. Top with a few leaves of fresh basil, and drizzle with balsamic vinegar and extra virgin olive oil. Finish with a pinch of salt.

Note . . . You can purchase beets already peeled and cooked. If you have a little time, however, try your hand at roasting fresh ones:

Preheat oven to 350°F. Slice off the stem and trim the very tip of each beetroot so that it can sit flat. Don't bother with peeling off the skin yet, but wash them well, rub with a little olive oil, and season to taste with salt and pepper. Place your beets in a baking dish big enough to spread them out in one layer, and add a small amount of water to the bottom of the pan. Cover tightly with aluminum to prevent the tops from burning, and roast in oven for 45 minutes to 1 hour. When you can press through the skin with a paring knife and the centers are tender, the beets are done. Remove them from the oven and let cool. When the beets have cooled, you can easily rub the skin off using a paper towel.

Reserved

## TRUFFLE CHEESE CROQUES with ONION

The French make an infamously rich grilled ham-and-cheese sandwich called a *croque monsieur*. Sometimes they'll crack an egg on it, and then it's called a *croque madame*. A simple appetizer, our cheese croque (pronounced "croak") got its name from this traditional snack. We then modified it using some other distinctly French flavors.

1 to 2 tablespoons butter
1 sweet white onion,
  finely diced
Salt
Truffle oil (optional)

Sliced white or buttermilk
  bread
2 to 3 ounces truffle cheese,
  sliced thinly (see Note)

Melt the butter in a sauté pan over low heat. Add onion to pan, lightly salt, and cook, covered, until it becomes clear and soft. (This always takes less heat and more time than you think.) Remove from heat. Toss the sweated onion with just a few drops of truffle oil, if using.

Butter one side each of two slices of bread. Spread a couple spoonfuls of the onion mixture on an unbuttered side of bread. Layer with truffle cheese. Sandwich together with the other slice of bread and place your sandwich, buttered sides out, in the pan. Armed with low heat and patience, melt the cheese completely and brown both sides of bread.

Remove the croque from the pan, slice into quarters, and serve.

Note . . . Masquerading as mushrooms, truffles happen to be a particularly delicious type of mold. They are rare and expensive, as is any food with extremely specialized growing conditions and the inability to be harvested mechanically.

To have a look at mushrooms of all seasons, turn to page 121 ☞

---

☞ GOURMET VS. GOURMAND: A *gourmet* is a connoisseur of fine food and drink. A *gourmand* is a person who is fond of good eating, often indiscriminately and to excess.

For a few anecdotes from a true gourmand, turn to page 74 ☜

A *NEW YORK TIMES* ARTICLE FROM JUNE 10, 1900, SHEDS
LIGHT ON THE EARLIEST OF RECIPES:

To the Romans belongs the honor of having produced the
first European cookery book; and, though the authorship
is uncertain, it is generally attributed to Caelius Apicius,
who lived under Trajan (A.D. 114). Here are two recipes
from the ancient collection: "First, for a sauce to be eaten
with boiled fowl, put the following ingredients into a mortar: aniseed, dried mint, and lazer root. Cover them with
vinegar, add dates, and pour in liquamen (a distilled liquor
made from large fish which were salted and allowed to
turn putrid in the sun), oil, and a small quantity of mustard
seeds. Reduce all to a proper thickness with sweet wine
warmed, and then pour this same over your chicken, which
should previously be boiled in aniseed water." The second
recipe shows the same queer mixture of ingredients: "Take
a wheelbarrow of rose leaves and pound in a mortar, add
to it brains of two pigs and two thrushes boiled and mixed
with the chopped-up yolk of egg, oil, vinegar, pepper, and
wine. Mix and pour these together, and stew them steadily
and slowly till the perfume is developed."

The Romans were very fond of surprise dishes, such as
pigs stuffed with live thrushes; and, to anticipate a little,
this taste descended so near our own times as the reign of
Charles II, as witness a recipe of that date for making two

pies which were to be served together—one containing live birds and the other live frogs. When the latter was opened "out skip the frogs, which make the ladies to shriek and skip," while the birds when released were to add to the general confusion by flying at the candles and putting out the lights. A dish of peacock was a favorite plat at Rome, and was served at the beginning of dinner. The bird, having first been done to death by stifling, was then skinned; the inside was filled with the flesh of other birds, and the whole sewn together, and finally sent in to table affixed to a small branch as if alive.

In general, mankind, since the improvement in cookery, eats twice as much as nature requires.

☞ BENJAMIN FRANKLIN

## STEAK TARTARE

Yes, steak tartare is, in fact, chopped raw meat. This dish has been around since medieval times, first made popular by the aptly named Tartars, a Turkic tribe; the Tartars would shred low-quality portions of precious beef so none would be wasted. There is a myth that they would also put freshly cut meat under their saddles in order to tenderize it as they rode from place to place.

The practice of mixing ground beef with spices didn't come until the dish was introduced to Germany, where it was consumed both raw and cooked. The cooked version became quite popular, and in 1850s New York, ground beef patties were sold on the street by a German immigrant who hailed from a small town by the name of Hamburg . . .

Serve variations on this popular patty at your next party using the bite-size recipes on page 133 ☞

Essential to steak tartare are three seasonings: parsley, mustard, and black pepper. Tartare looks and tastes best when minced by hand. Make sure the meat is cold enough to chop cleanly without tearing. Ideally, when chopped it should look like coarsely ground beef. A shy hand with the seasonings will create a dish that is unmemorable.

Toasted pumpernickel is a classic accompaniment. A sliced olive baguette, toasted with a little olive oil, works great as well.

At Bix we always feature seasonal produce, and one of our favorite ingredients, though often overlooked, are fresh mushrooms. We include them in a variety of dishes at every time of the year. Special thanks are due to Connie Green, owner of Wine Forest Wild Mushrooms, and the foragers who make it possible to get the highest quality product.

**SPRING**..................................................................porcini
**SUMMER**................................................................morels
**EARLY FALL**........................................................chanterelles
**LATE FALL**........................................................winter porcini

Another not-so-subtle seasonal delight at Bix? Heirloom tomatoes on their very own rolling cart. See page 131 ☞

## PIGS IN A BLANKET

Admit it, you love them: franks in a jacket, biscuit dogs, kilted sausages, corndogs. There is a similar English dish called "toad-in-the-hole" that involves cooking sausages, then baking them in batter. The Czechs make a *klobasnek* by filling flaky, sweet pastry dough with sausage. Whenever we pass them around any gathering at the restaurant, they are always the most popular hors d'oeuvre. Unless you're adept at charcuterie, buy your pigs at the market; puff pastry—flaky, buttery, and fast cooking—makes great blankets.

Puff pastry comes in sheets, often frozen, so look in the freezer section of your supermarket. Once you open the package and let the dough thaw, you'll find it is often marked with perforations for you to pull it apart into smaller pieces. If not, cut 2-by-2-inch squares of dough. Then cut each square in half, from corner to corner, to form two triangles. Wrap one triangle around a hot dog, set the pigs on a lightly greased cookie sheet, and bake according to the directions on the puff pastry package.

A highbrow is the kind of person who looks at a sausage and thinks of Picasso.

☛ SIR ALAN PATRICK HERBERT

Smoking meat or fish is easy to do, and it's hard to beat the aroma and flavor you can add to a dish simply by getting creative with the grill. You'll find hardwood chips and chunks in cookware shops, supermarkets, your backyard, and even the pet store. Chips work best for quick-cooking foods, while chunks are better suited to smoking larger items. Soak either chips or chunks in water for an hour before using so they will smoke rather than burn when you throw them on top of the coals in your grill.

Softwoods such as pine and fir have too many oils, and there-fore burn too easily to use for smoking. Hardwoods commonly used for smoking include the following:

**HICKORY**................................................................ribs and red meats

**OAK, PECAN**......................................................................brisket

**ALDER**.......................................................any fish, especially salmon

**MESQUITE**................................................ribs, red meat, and poultry

**APPLE, ORANGE, CHERRY, OR MAPLE**...................poultry or ham

# SEASONAL PRODUCE

## WINTER FRUITS

Bananas
Clementines
Cranberries
Grapes (red)
Grapefruit
Kiwis
Kumquats

Oranges
Passion fruit
Pears
Pomegranates
Pomelos
Tangelos
Tangerines

## WINTER VEGETABLES

Artichokes
Avocados
Bok choy
Broccoli
Broccoli rabe
Brussels sprouts
Cabbage

Cauliflowers
Chestnuts
Kale
Lettuce
Parsnips
Radishes
Rutabagas

Snow peas                    Turnips
Squash, winter               Watercress
Sweet potatoes

## SPRING FRUITS

Apricots                     Papayas
Blueberries                  Pineapples
Cherries                     Strawberries

## SPRING VEGETABLES

Artichokes                   Onions
Asparagus                    Onions, green
Beans, fava                  Peas, English
Black chanterelles           Peas, sugar snap
Carrots                      Ramps
Fennel                       Rhubarb
Garlic, green                Scallions
Lettuce                      Spinach
Okra                         Swiss chard

# SEASONAL PRODUCE

## SUMMER FRUITS

Apricots
Asian pears
Blackberries
Blueberries
Cantaloupes
Casaba melons
Cherries
Crenshaw melons
Currants
Figs
Gooseberries
Grapes

Guava
Honeydew melons
Huckleberries
Lychees
Mangoes
Nectarines
Papayas
Peaches
Plums
Raspberries
Strawberries
Watermelons

## SUMMER VEGETABLES

Arugula
Avocados
Beans, green
Beets
Broccoli

Corn, sweet
Cucumbers
Eggplant
Garlic
Kohlrabi

Okra
Onions
Peas, English
Peppers, bell
Potatoes

Shallots
Squash, summer
Swiss chard
Tomatoes
Zucchini

## FALL FRUITS

Apples
Bananas
Cranberries
Grapes
Grapefruit
Kiwis

Kumquats
Oranges
Pears
Persimmons
Pomegranates
Quinces

Wish it was summer all year round? Go quench your thirst with the limey classic on page 40 and imagine yourself on the beach in tropical Havana

## FALL VEGETABLES

Avocados
Beans, shelling
Beets
Bok choy
Broccoli
Broccoli rabe
Brussels sprouts
Cabbage
Carrots
Cauliflower
Chestnuts
Collard greens
Garlic

Kale
Leeks
Lettuce
Parsnips
Peppers, gypsy, piquillo
Pumpkin
Rutabagas
Spinach
Squash, winter
Sweet potatoes
Swiss chard
Turnips
Watercress

A fruit is a vegetable with looks and money. Plus, if you let fruit rot, it turns to wine, something Brussels sprouts never do.

☞ P. J. O'ROURKE

Every year, starting in spring, we get calls asking if our tomato cart is up and running. We always have to tell overeager customers that it doesn't start until mid to late July (and continues through October). We slice a wide variety of heirloom tomatoes and serve them tableside from a rolling cart, giving customers the choice of eating their tomatoes with Maldon salt, freshly ground black pepper, chopped basil, balsamic vinegar, and olive oil. We pay particular attention to the olive oil, as we believe it to be the most important ingredient. For those who aren't satisfied with the freshest, ripest tomatoes on the market, we offer house-made mozzarella daily.

HEIRLOOM is a term applied to varieties of fruits, vegetables, and flowers grown from open-pollinated cultivars—that is to say, not hybrids or plants that need to be pollinated by hand. These varieties are called "heirlooms" because they were once widely grown but decreased in popularity with the rise of commercial agriculture. The most commonly known heirloom fruit is the tomato. There are hundreds of varieties, each possessing a different size, color, shape, taste, and texture.

Looking for an ice-cold beverage to go along with your summery tomatoes? Why not try one found on page 23 🐟

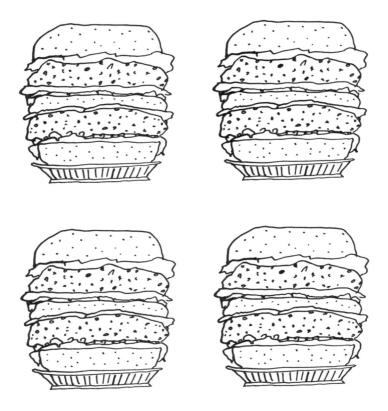

# MINI HAMBURGERS with ACCOMPANIMENTS

They're tiny! They're great for passing! You can eat them in one bite! The difficult thing about mini burgers? Well, they're tiny. Making the patty is actually the simple part—the tricky thing is finding a bun small enough for a bite-sized portion. We bake our own gougères, savory French pastry puffs made with Gruyère cheese. Short of making your own gougères, any sturdy bread can be stamped into bite-sized rounds with a small biscuit cutter. Toasted rye or pumpernickel work well.

Loosely form 1 pound of raw meat into plump patties approximately 1½ inches across. Fry or grill until the meat reaches the desired temperature.

## ACCOMPANIMENTS FOR THE MINI BURGERS

There are a lot of different condiment options with surprising flavors that you can offer your guests. The payoff for making tiny hamburgers is that you can try all the toppings on the table. Here are three simple ideas to get you started.

## BLUE CHEESE DRESSING

Mix together in a bowl 5 ounces of crumbled blue cheese with 2 tablespoons of mayonnaise and 2 tablespoons of buttermilk.

## CARAMELIZED ONIONS

Slice one medium-size white or yellow onion. Place 2 tablespoons of butter in a pan set over low heat, and add the onion when the butter is melted. Leave the onion in the pan, stirring regularly—the lower the heat, the better. First, the onion will turn clear. Slowly, its sugars will start to caramelize, and the onion will then start taking on a golden color. The secret to making good onions is to constantly scrape the brown bits that start sticking to the pan back into the mixture. These onions are done when they've turned a dark amber brown. One onion, prepared in this manner, should take you about 45 minutes. Let cool slightly, then spread directly onto the hamburger bun.

## CLASSIC GARLIC AIOLI

Aioli—homemade mayonnaise with lots of garlic—takes a bit of finesse and a good food processor. A few tips: First, let all of your ingredients come to room temperature, as this makes it easier for them to combine. Second, when adding the oil to the egg yolk, go slow. Take until next Bastille Day if you have to, but when aioli recipes say "add a drop at a time" they really mean a drop at a time. Once you see that the mixture has changed texture and begun to emulsify, you can begin adding the oil in a steady stream. Ultimately, you can flavor aioli with any herb or spice. Basil, Dijon mustard, and harissa (a spicy North African pepper paste) work well. You can also experiment with any flavor or type of olive oil you like.

| | |
|---|---|
| 1 clove garlic, chopped | 2 teaspoons fresh lemon juice |
| 1 teaspoon salt, plus more to taste | 2 cups olive oil |
| 2 egg yolks | Freshly ground black pepper |

Begin by crushing your garlic and salt with a mortar and pestle. Mix in the egg yolk and lemon juice, and then add the mixture to the food processor. Combine. Begin to slowly add the olive oil,

134

a few drops at a time, through the feeder tube while the food processor is running. Once the mixture begins to thicken, you can add the oil in a thin stream. Season with salt and pepper to taste. If the mixture becomes too thick, add a few drops of water to keep it from separating.

Note . . . Many restaurants offer flavored mayonnaises and call them "aioli," but what defines this traditional French sauce is the garlic.

Fans of tiny food may wish to turn to page 139 ☛

Oysters are a great party food. They are uncommon, special, and completely idiot-proof. All you have to do it buy them—the ocean has already done the rest. Oysters have amazing *terroir*, that is to say, their flavor is strongly influenced by the conditions in which they're raised. Oysters from the East Coast tend to be milder, because they are grown in the flat waters of the Atlantic. They are also grown completely submerged in water, which means their shells are smoother. Pacific oysters are grown both in and out of coastal waters, and the constant fight against the tide lends ridges to their shells and a distinctive, robust flavor.

## A FEW OYSTER TIPS

**1.** Oysters should be eaten alive. If the shell is open, tap it to see if it closes. If not, it's dead. Don't eat it. A fresh oyster will feel heavier than it looks.

**2.** Oysters can be stored in the fridge for a short amount of time underneath a wet towel for moisture. Ideally, they should be eaten as soon as possible.

**3.** Oysters should have all of their liquor (liquid). If one feels light or is stored lengthwise in the store (allowing the juice to run out), pass.

## HOW TO SHUCK AN OYSTER

Perhaps the only obstacle to serving oysters is opening them. For some reason, these creatures have an aversion to being pried open with cold steel. We recommend you get an oyster knife, which has a thick handle and a blunted point and is sold anywhere you can buy fresh oysters. This is a case of having the right tool for the right job.

**1.** Wear a glove or hold the oyster in a folded towel to protect your hand. In the process of opening the bivalve, you're going to try to keep the liquor inside, which is most easily done by resting it upright (rounded side down) against the countertop while you hold the shell. Insert your knife at the rear of the shell where it is hinged shut.

**2.** Work the knife into the shell, taking your time. You'll feel the knife slowly slide in, and eventually you should be far enough to give it a twist. You will hear the shell pop. Pull out your knife and wipe the bits of shell on your towel. This prevents them from getting stuck to the oyster meat on the inside.

**3.** Insert the knife back into the shell, angling it upward. You're looking to sever the muscle that connects the two halves of the shell, located toward the front, without damaging the oyster meat. You'll know when you've got it—the two halves will come right apart.

**4.** Time to cut the oyster free. Slide your knife underneath the meat and separate it from the knob that connects it to the bottom of the shell. Check for any large grit or bits of cracked shell before serving.

**5.** Serve with a few drops of lemon juice or our classic favorite, a Mignonette sauce.

## MIGNONETTE SAUCE

¼ cup Champagne vinegar
¾ cup white wine
1 tablespoon minced shallots

1 teaspoon cracked black
pepper

Mix all ingredients together and serve with oysters on the half shell.

Note . . . A tiny trick of the Bix kitchen: Toasting your peppercorns will yield much more fragrant spice. Pop them in a 350°F oven for 10 minutes. Also, rather than putting them in a grinder, try cracking them with the back of a heavy skillet to achieve a much coarser texture, suitable for Mignonette sauce.

# MAKING FOOD SMALLER: A BRIEF LEXICON

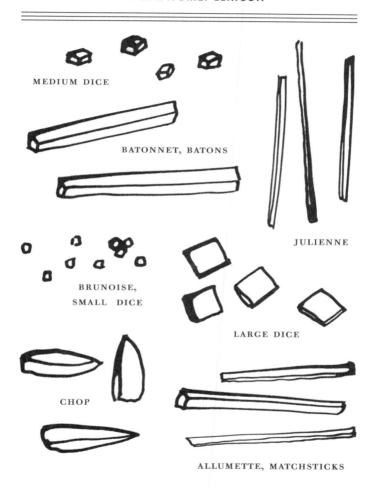

MEDIUM DICE

BATONNET, BATONS

JULIENNE

BRUNOISE,
SMALL DICE

LARGE DICE

CHOP

ALLUMETTE, MATCHSTICKS

## CHOOSE YOUR WEAPON

PARING

FILET

CLEAVER

UTILITY

CHEF'S

BREAD

Three essential kitchen knives:

**CHEF'S KNIFE:** Your most essential tool, whose usefulness is rivaled only by fire and the wheel. The wedge-shaped blade of a chef's knife is key to quickly chopping food without hitting your hand on the countertop. Look for a blade at least 8 inches long.

**PARING KNIFE:** Let's face it, you will eventually have to peel something, probably something irritatingly small or slippery. The paring knife, with its 3-inch blade, is here to help.

**BREAD KNIFE:** The serrated edge of a bread knife is designed to prevent you from mangling a perfectly harmless loaf of bread. It can also handle anything with a tough exterior and soft interior.

Three splurges for wreaking specialized culinary havoc:

**UTILITY KNIFE:** Shorter and thinner than a chef's knife, a 6-inch utility knife is great for slicing soft foods like sandwiches, fruits, and cheeses.

**CLEAVER:** A hefty, square-bladed knife designed for hacking through cartilage and bones.

**FILLET KNIFE:** The signature element to this blade is its sharpness and flexibility, which is required to effectively fillet a fish. The length can range from 4 inches to 9 inches.

**CARDAMOM:** Cardamom is native to India and Sri Lanka, although Guatemala is now the biggest exporter of the spice. Cardamom pods ripen at different times, which makes their harvest particularly labor intensive. When purchasing cardamom, make sure you buy it still in the pod, as it has an almost nuclear half-life—it loses its essential oils at a rate of about 40 percent a year.

**VANILLA:** Translations for the Spanish word *vainilla* range anywhere from "little pod" to "little vagina," which goes a long way toward explaining the superstition in Elizabethan England that the spice—the long fruit of a tropical orchid—held bewitching aphrodisiac powers. Vanilla is native to the eastern coast of Mexico, though most of the world's vanilla is now produced in Madagascar.

**SAFFRON:** The hand-picked stamens of *Crocus sativus*, saffron is so expensive because it can take anywhere from 70,000 to 250,000 flowers to produce one pound of dried spice. There is evidence that saffron has been widely prized for more than four thousand years and has been used to treat more than ninety different illnesses. Common substitutions include safflower stamens and dried turmeric.

**Q:** Where do we get the word *marshmallow*?

A. Queen Elizabeth's personal pastry chef, Edmund J. Mallow

B. An African herb traditionally used in medicine

C. A corruption of the English word *tallow*, which, when melted in vats for candle making, resembled the confection

D. Genmallow, an early substitute for vanilla

See answer, page 156

Love sugar? Get to know it better on page 147

# BIX'S HOMEMADE VANILLA ICE CREAM

Making your own ice cream from a personal recipe is one of the simplest ways to make a common commodity special. It's so simple, in fact, there are machines that will make the ice cream for you. So toss in some ingredients, flip the switch, and watch your guests await in eager anticipation.

| | |
|---|---|
| 2½ cups heavy cream | 2 tablespoons mascarpone |
| 1½ cups milk | 1¼ cups sugar |
| ½ cup egg yolks (approximately 6 to 7 eggs) | Seeds from ½ vanilla bean (see Note) |

Place all ingredients in an ice cream maker. Switch the machine on. Follow the manufacturer's recommendations on how long to keep the machine churning. Most ice cream benefits from an hour or so in the freezer after it's done.

Note . . . You'll have to scrape the vanilla seeds out of the bean before committing it to the machine. Lay the pod on a cutting board, and trim both ends. Slice halfway through the pod, lengthwise, and then you should be able to open it up. Scrape out the seeds to use in your recipe. You can also include the whole bean in the ice cream as it's mixing for more flavor—just pull out the pod before putting the ice cream in the freezer.

Vanilla is one of the most labor-intensive spices to harvest, along with the two others found on page 142 ⌐

# TYPES OF SUGARS IN FOOD

**GLUCOSE**..............................................................found in grapes, blood

**FRUCTOSE**...........................................................found in fruit, honey

**GALACTOSE**.......................................................found in milk, brains

**LACTOSE**............................................................1 molecule of glucose +
1 molecule of galactose, found in milk

**MALTOSE**........................................2 attached molecules of glucose
found in germinating grains

**SUCROSE**......................................................1 molecule of glucose +
1 molecule of fructose, found in milk

---

☞ Not even sugar is immune to gravity; fruit is always sweeter at the end hanging closest to the ground.

## FRUITS THAT RIPEN AFTER PICKING

Apples

Apricots

Avocados

Bananas

Blueberries

Figs

Guavas

Honeydew melons

Kiwis

Mangos

Muskmelons

Nectarines

Papayas

Passion fruit

Peaches

Pears

Persimmons

Plantains

Plums

Quinces

Tomatoes

## FRUITS THAT DON'T

Blackberries

Cherries

Lemons

Limes

Oranges

Grapefruits

Grapes

Pineapples

Pomegranates

Raspberries

Strawberries

Watermelons

# STRAWBERRY SHAPES

OBLATE

NECKED

GLOBOSE

GLOBOSE CONIC

SHORT WEDGE

LONG WEDGE

CONIC

LONG CONIC

## STRAWBERRY PARFAIT

Strawberries in season are the perfect food—fresh, sweet, universally likable, easy to prepare. Serving them can be as simple or as complicated as you wish. Displaying your fruit in a clever vessel, such as a white-wine glass, instantly disguises the lack of work you put into preparing it. Here are three ways to dress strawberries, in order of lack of difficulty:

### STRAWBERRIES WITH BROWN-SUGAR CREAM

In a mixer, beat together 1 cup of heavy cream with 1¼ tablespoons brown sugar until stiff peaks form. Hull fresh, ripe strawberries. Top the berries with cream.

### STRAWBERRIES WITH BROWN-SUGAR-AND-COGNAC CREAM

Add a splash of cognac to the above recipe before whipping.

### STRAWBERRIES WITH ZINFANDEL AND AGAVE GLAZE

Combine 2 cups of red Zinfandel with 1 cup agave nectar (see Note) in a pan over medium-low heat until the liquid reduces by about half; it should become syrupy. Pour over strawberries while warm, or chill in the freezer and use as a topping for berries and ice cream.

Note . . . Agave nectar is a relatively new product in the United States, made from the nectar of the same Weber cactus from which we distill tequila and prepared the same way as maple syrup. An all-natural sweetener with a lower glycemic index than sucrose and slightly less viscosity than corn syrup, agave nectar is becoming less and less difficult to find. The cooks at Bix have tried it in recipes like sorbet, peanut brittle, and caramel. It can easily be added to a Margarita in place of other sweeteners. Strangely—or perhaps predictably—some commercial producers have started mixing the nectar with high-fructose corn syrup, much in the way cheap tequila is blended with rum to stretch the product. Just like tequila, make sure the bottle you buy is clearly labeled "100 percent pure agave."

Still curious about cactus? Turn to page 44 ⌐█

The traditional way to drink vodka is ice-cold and served neat in a frozen glass. For an effective, dramatic way to keep your beverage ice-cold, cut the top off a half-gallon milk carton, place a bottle of vodka inside, fill the carton with water, and set in the freezer. When it's time to serve the vodka, simply cut away the milk carton and your bottle will be encased in its own block of ice. Serve neat in a tiny stemmed glass with a lemon twist, or pour a shot over a few scoops of lemon sorbet.

Note . . . It sounds counterintuitive, but fill your carton with hot water, which should enhance the clarity of the ice. Ideally you should be able to read the label of the bottle through it.

**Q:** Combining wintergreen, vanilla, and cassia (a form of cinnamon) gives us what flavor?

A. Wintermint

B. Bubblegum

C. Allspice

D. Licorice

See answer, page 156

# LAST CALL

Though we've tried to add a touch of sophistication to our neighborhood, Gold Street wasn't always so civilized. The August 23, 1850, edition of the *Daily Alta California*, a historical San Francisco newspaper, states: "According to the report of M. Fallon, the city marshal, to the Grand Jury, the number of arrests made in San Francisco by the police between the 13TH of November, 1849, and the 1ST of August, 1850, were classified as follows:

MURDER..................................................................................7

LARCENY.............................................................................230

BURGLARY...............................................................................6

ASSAULT.............................................................................102

PERJURY.................................................................................1

ROBBERY.................................................................................3

DESERTIONS...........................................................................50

MUTINY.................................................................................18

DRUNKENESS.........................................................................581

RESISTING OF OFFICERS...........................................................8

SWINDLING..............................................................................5

THREATENING TO TAKE LIFE.....................................................14

PICKING POCKETS.....................................................................4

CONSPIRACY............................................................................2

BREACH OF PEACE.....................................................................6

ACTING POLICY OFFICER............................................................4

SUSPICION OF FREEING CRIMINALS............................................2

DELIRIUM TREMENS...................................................................5

What ordinary libation allegedly incites to crime? Turn to page 46 to find out Turn to page 46 to find out 🖛

## THE ANSWERS YOU SEEK

From page 37
**D:** Rob Roy

From page 55
**C:** Mae West

From page 105
**C:** Muddy Waters

From page 109
**D:** The Cantalupo was a papal summer estate near Rome.

From page 143
**B:** The "marsh mallow" is a plant native to Africa. Its roots were used in colonial times to flavor the confection of the same name.

From page 152
**B:** Bubblegum

## ACKNOWLEDGMENTS

Several of the recipes in this book are on the menu at Bix, some are not, but we have our hardworking, talented kitchen staff to thank for all the tips and tricks herein—they are responsible for transforming that grilled-cheese sandwich into a truffled croque.

Our chef and partner, Bruce Hill, deserves his own cookbook. In the meantime, he offers only this piece of advice: "Good food starts with good ingredients."

For twenty years of hard work and dedication behind the plank, a very special thank-you is extended to Bruce Minkewicz and Bradley Avey, Bix's original barmen.

Music has been a tremendous influence on this restaurant, and many gifted musicians have given us years of their expertise, especially Mary Stallings, George Khouri, and Don Asher.

Thanks to our associates Bill Higgins and Bill Upson.

In fond remembrance of Luigi and Roberto. We miss you.

# THE FINE PRINT

Angostura bitters is a registered trademark of Angostura International; Aperol aperitif is a registered trademark of Davide Campari Milano S.P.A.; Beefeater gin is a registered trademark of Allied Domecq Spirits & Wine, Ltd.; Bombay Sapphire gin is a registered trademark of Bacardi & Company, Ltd.; Boodles gin is a registered trademark of Chivas Brothers Pernod Ricard; Calvados brandy is a registered trademark of Calvados Boulard; Campari aperitif is a registered trademark of Davide Campari Milano S.P.A.; Carpano Antica vermouth is a registered trademark of G. B. Carpano S.R.L.; Chartreuse liqueur is a registered trademark of Chartreuse Corp.; Chopin vodka is a registered trademark of Podlaska Wytwornia Wodek "Polmos" Spolka Akcyjna; Clavinet keyboard is a registered trademark of Hohner, Inc.; Coca-Cola soda is a registered trademark of the Coca-Cola Company; Cointreau liqueur is a registered trademark of Cointreau Corp.; Coke soda is a registered trademark of the Coca-Cola Company; Cristal Champagne is a registered trademark of Champagne Louis Roederer; Damrak gin is a registered trademark of Distilleerderijen Erven Lucas Bols B.V.; Dom Pérignon Champagne is a registered trademark of Moët Hennessy USA, Inc.; Excedrin analgesic is a registered trademark of Novartis AG; Fernet-Branca liqueur is a registered trademark of Fratelli Branca Distillerie S.R.L., Ltd.; Flor de Caña rum is a registered trademark of Compania Licorera de Centroamerica, S.A.; Germain-Robin Alambic Brandy is a registered trademark of Alambic, Inc.; Grammy Award is a registered trademark of National Academy of Recording Arts & Sciences, Inc.; Gran Torres liqueur is a registered trademark of Miguel Torres, S.A.; Grand Marnier liqueur is a registered trademark of Societe des Produits Marnier-Lapostolle; Havana Club rum is a registered trademark of Havana Club Holding S.A.; Hendrick's gin is a registered trademark of William Grant & Sons, Inc.; Herbsaint liquor is a registered trademark of the Sazerac Company, Inc.; Jägermeister digestif is a registered trademark of Mast-Jagermeister Aktiengesellschaft Corp.; Lillet aperitif is a registered trademark of Societe Lillet Freres Corp.; Luksusowa vodka is a registered trademark of Lubuska Wytwornia Wodek Gatunkowych Polmos S.A.; Luxardo Maraschino Liqueur is a registered trademark of Girolamo Luxardo S.P.A.; Pernod liqueur is a registered trademark of

Pernod Ricard; Peychaud's bitters is a registered trademark of the Sazerac Company, Inc.; Pimm's liqueur is a registered trademark of Diageo Brands B.V.; Pimm's No. 1 liqueur is a registered trademark of Diageo Brands B.V.; Plymouth gin is a registered trademark of V&S Vin & Sprit Aktiebolag; Punt e Mes vermouth is a registered trademark of G. B. Carpano S.R.L.; Ricard liqueur is a registered trademark of Pernod Ricard; Sazerac whiskey is a registered trademark of the Sazerac Company, Inc.; Smirnoff liquors is a registered trademark of Diageo North America, Inc.; Sriracha Chili Sauce is a registered trademark of Huy Fong Foods, Inc.; Tanqueray gin is a registered trademark of Diageo Brands B.V.; Tanqueray No. Ten gin is a registered trademark of Diageo Brands B.V.

## FAMOUS LAST WORDS

I should have never switched from Scotch to Martinis.

☞ HUMPHREY BOGART, ACTOR
DIED JANUARY 14, 1957

That was a great game of golf, fellers.

☞ HARRY LILLIS "BING" CROSBY, SINGER/ACTOR
DIED OCTOBER 14, 1977

I've had a hell of a lot of fun and I've enjoyed every minute of it.

☞ ERROL FLYNN, ACTOR
DIED OCTOBER 14, 1959

God will pardon me, that's his line of work.

☞ HEINRICH HEINE, POET
DIED FEBRUARY 15, 1856

Here am I, dying of a hundred good symptoms.

☞ ALEXANDER POPE, WRITER
DIED MAY 30, 1744

I've had eighteen straight whiskies. I think that's the record.

☞ DYLAN THOMAS, POET
DIED NOVEMBER 9, 1953

Either that wallpaper goes, or I do.

☞ OSCAR WILDE, WRITER
DIED NOVEMBER 30, 1900